To Mike Harmer:
A fine teacher who believed it could happen.

And to Beth:
My wonderful wife, who made it happen.

MAJORING IN LIFE

MAJORING
in Life

MANFRED KOEHLER

SERVANT PUBLICATIONS
ANN ARBOR, MICHIGAN

Vine Books is an imprint of Servant Publications especially designed to serve evangelical Christians.

Published by Servant Publications
P.O. Box 8617
Ann Arbor, Michigan 48107

Cover design byUttley/DouPonce DesignWorks, Sisters, Oregon

02 03 04 05 10 9 8 7 6 5 4 3

Printed in the United States of America
ISBN 1-56955-286-X

Contents

Preface
(You may want to read this.)

The World Trade Center. The Pentagon. Columbine. Oklahoma City. The tragic events of recent history have dramatically changed your life, your world, and your future. This book seeks to point you to someone who *does not change:* Jesus Christ. He is the same yesterday, today, and forever (Hebrews 13:8). You need him now as never before.

The following pages were not written to be read cover to cover. Like lights along a garden pathway, each chapter stands alone, ready to help point the way wherever you may be. Feel free to pick and choose accordingly.

This book is full of stories. A few are pure fabrication, yarns from the mind of a wordsmith who loves to read and write fiction. Others are autobiographical, windows into my sometimes anguished soul. Some are true tales from recent graduates. I've modified the details to protect both the innocent and the guilty, whatever the case may be.

This book does not profess to be the definitive answer to any of the challenges that face you beyond graduation. There's only one Book that can truly make that claim. With that in mind, have your Bible with you as you read. Look up the Scripture passages these pages point you to and consider them. There's no rush. If this book contains any valid conclusions, allow God's Word to make them your own. And equally as important, you'll need the Bible to unmask my unintended errors. Be a noble Berean (Acts 17:11).

Having said that, I humbly but confidently present you with a book I wish someone had written before I graduated from North Park High. Life's road would have been a whole lot easier to negotiate.

1

Seeing Jesus at Your Graduation

(Counting on Christ to be there tomorrow)

Nervous smiles gave them away.

They stood in royal blue gowns, grad caps neatly donned, gold tassels swinging circles by each right ear. Friends and family from all over the United States and Canada fanned out before them, eager to watch the ceremony. Graduate scrolls lay in a tidy row on an oak table beside the podium. Principal, master of ceremonies, and graduation speaker had arrived on time. The five soon-to-be graduates stood tall, cool, and collected. Finely brushed teeth gleamed under the platform lights.

But those smiles looked just a little forced.

Stefanie was thinking about a career in journalism, but she wondered if she had the wherewithal to pull it off as a writer. She had applied to Columbia Bible College, never having had a chance to set foot on campus. Her boyfriend was way off in Oregon, so she had no idea where that relationship was going. And Mom and Dad were missionaries—they'd be an inexpensive phone call away.

For Stefanie, high school graduation spelled *uncertainty*.

Kyle looked forward to a simple job and no responsibility. He had vague dreams of forming a band and hanging out with friends in some bachelor apartment in northern Manitoba. Mostly he just wanted to be away from home, to make some of his own decisions for a while. He didn't have a clue what God wanted.

All Kyle knew was that, right now, graduation meant *freedom*.

Claire groaned at the core every time she thought of her family. Her best friends were her kid sister, Mom, and Dad. Her first step after graduation would be Nepal—a summer missions trip. After that, she was enrolled in a photography program in Vermont. But her "best friends" were a long way from Vermont, let alone Nepal. May as well have been Venus or Neptune.

To Claire, graduation would cost her dearly in terms of *separation*.

Darren loved people—especially girls. And people, especially the girls, loved Darren. He couldn't believe he'd come to the end of his high school years without a serious girlfriend. Nor could any of the girls. Darren wasn't a playboy; he just wanted to be loved, get married, and have a family. Yesterday.

Darren hoped that after graduation he'd find some new *opportunities*.

Rob's dream was to fly. He'd filled in his Air Force Academy applications, visions of *Top Gun* buzzing through his cranium at Mach 2, but he still hadn't heard. He was afraid his eyesight might be a factor. Money scared him, too—or the lack of it. His parents didn't have much, so he'd have to fend for himself financially. How much could a high school escapee make in a summer, anyway?

Rob was certain graduation went hand in hand with *fear*.

Fighting through the fog of surreal thoughts the occasion forced on them, the five looked up as the graduation speaker rose. Ears perked, they waited, hoping he had something relevant to say.

You've come to the end of a long road, the speaker began. *It's had happy times and hard times. Your parents have prayed you through the pilgrimage, your teachers have walked beside you, and your friends have shared the adventures. Now, one more step and you're done. The cameras will flash. Your parents will cry. Your teachers will smile. Your friends will say a sad good-bye.*

Claire glanced over at her family, heart lurching.

But your last step in this journey is only the first in your next. The sky of opportunity spreads cloudless before you. Adulthood awaits your direction, your choices, your ambition.

And life is about to become more complicated.

Stefanie shook her head. This was *not* what she wanted to hear.

Enemies lurk ahead. Satan prowls like a lion, hungry for your youth, your potential, your very life. The world seeks to snag you in its claws and transfix your mind in its grip. And the enemy you've already long fought—yourself, your flesh—will continue its feverish battle to the death.

Your parents' love, your teachers' prayers, and your friends' care will follow as you face this scary unknown. Each of those is an incredibly valuable gift. But you need someone else, someone greater, someone who's always there.

That someone is Jesus.

He is your Savior, Friend, Counselor, and King. He craves to be your all in all. He's much more than your ticket to paradise. He's your very life.

It's his wisdom that will guide you through the caverns of this world. It's his hand you'll fall into when temptation trips you up. It's his patience that will endure when you've given up on yourself. It's his faithfulness that will stand tall when disappointment surrounds you. It's his strength that will uphold your soul when all else tumbles down.

Sure, great. Darren wondered if Jesus could just find him a girlfriend.

Remember: He walked Calvary's lonely trail so you would never walk alone. He poured out his life so yours could be full. He was wounded so you could be whole. His blood is your forgiveness. His cross is your freedom. He still bears the scars. Run your finger along the rough rim of each nail-pierced hole. Stick a hand in his side. Don't ever forget.

Set your eyes on Jesus.

You need him more than you know. Look at him; he's altogether lovely. Study him; you'll find his face in Scripture's every page. Cling to him; he cannot be moved. Listen to his voice; the universe knows none sweeter. Jesus is your light; stand in his glow. He's your resurrection; live in his hope. He's your bread; feast heartily at his table. He's your truth; look no further. He's your life; live him to the full. He's your way; enjoy the breathtaking tour.

Fix your heart on Jesus.

He's your gentle Shepherd, the Door to safety, your Entrance to the fold. Run to him when no one else understands. Hide in him when everything seems horrible. Warm your soul in him when all goes cold. Whatever your need, he'll be there. He always delivers, right on time.

Rob smiled, imagining Jesus running deliveries to him in a UPS truck. Better still, a Brink's armored car.

God's Son is your love. Jesus is your joy. Emmanuel is your peace. The Son of Man is patience, kindness, goodness. The Alpha and Omega is faithfulness, gentleness, and self-control. By enjoying Christ, you are all of these. When your soul lacks such beauty, ask for more of Jesus. Own him. Embrace him. Then stand to one side, so he can live.

Build your future on Jesus.

Christ, your Captain, has given you his armor. Cinch truth firmly to your soul. He's fitted you with a breastplate. Let his righteousness protect your heart from the evil one's accusations. Jesus has shod you with his shoes. Take each step in peace. Walk the Good News wherever you go. He's assigned you a shield, forged by your faith. Bear it courageously, consistently, and watch it quench the devil's darts. Christ has handed you a helmet. Allow his salvation to fill and protect your mind. He's armed you with a sword. Learn to wield it like a master, like your Master.

Kyle wrestled with the concept. He liked the idea of battle, but he wasn't sure he wanted a master—not even one as friendly as Jesus.

Having equipped you, your Commander sends you out as a soldier. Discover your mission soon. Join the ranks. Fight a good fight. And acknowledge your Captain's close presence at every step in the battle, with every stroke of your sword, and after every victory he grants you.

Go forward in Jesus.

Greatest of all, Christ's blood has provided you a telephone called prayer. The hotline to headquarters is always open. No operator, no answering machine, no long-distance static. Reinforcement is yours for the calling. God himself hears on the first ring.

In fact, Jesus is praying for you. He runs this race with you. He stands over, under, and around you. He lives within. He walks beside. He goes before. He's waiting, his arms open wide. He yearns to greet you with the words, "Well done, you good and faithful servant." That's a welcome you don't want to miss.

Congratulations. Your graduation is here. Your friends and family are proud of you, and they love you dearly.

But remember, Jesus loves you infinitely more. Go—and grow—in his grace.

With an encouraging nod and a smile, the speaker sat down.

The five grads weren't sure what to think. The words sounded true, but they didn't know what to do with them. Jesus was their Savior—all five were sure of that—but would he really be there in the challenges that now faced them? Was Jesus relevant in the adult world that waited? Was Jesus really all they needed?

That graduation speaker and this book make the same assumption: Yes, Jesus is relevant. And yes, he is all you need. Christ can answer your *uncertainties*, guide you into true *freedom*, alleviate the pain of *separation*, make the most of your *opportunities*, and tranquilize your *fears*. Jesus is not only about heaven in the distant hereafter; Jesus is about your future on earth here and now.

Congratulations. You're a graduate. But you're not ready to face the world on your own. You need Jesus. More.

2

A FedEx From Heaven?

(A fresh look at knowing God's will)

Stan sat staring into an empty Starbucks cup. His pencil, gnawed down to half its original length, spun absently between three fingers. A pad of paper lay before him, several words scratched haphazardly across its face: *University of Waterloo? Trinity College? Diane? Carol?*

Do you even care, God? The anguished prayer screamed silently upward. *Couldn't you just FedEx me from heaven so I'll know what you want?*

A burst of hard laughter filled the coffee shop. Cringing, Stan recognized several guys from his youth group. So much for sorting out his future in privacy. He closed his eyes, hoping it would make him invisible. The pencil stopped spinning.

"Yo, Stan, doing homework?" That had to be Ken Billings, the chunky, overblown comedian. "Get a clue, man. It's July. You've graduated. Homework is history."

Stan nodded, eyes still closed. He could hear the rustle of bodies around him, followed by the scrape of a chair. Suddenly, the midget pencil was torn from his fingers. Stan's eyes snapped open. Ken had the pencil in his mouth, chomping away where Stan had left off.

And the pad was in Ken's hands.

"Well, what do we have here?"

Stan tensed, stretching across the table to snatch back his pad, but Ken held it out of his reach.

"Whoa, not so fast. *University of Waterloo?* Where's that?"

There was the temptation to say nothing, but Ken could badger a guy to death. "Canada."

Ken began humming "O Canada," pencil bobbing inside a greasy smile, fat hand holding the pad for all to see. "Check this out, guys: *Diane and Carol.* Heh-heh. I think we know who Carol is. Isn't she going to Trinity College?"

Several heads nodded.

"But who's this Diane?" Ken leered across the table.

Stan clamped his mouth shut.

"She wouldn't be that sweet girl you met in Canada, would she?"

Stan stared into the empty Starbucks cup, shrinking under curious grins.

"She wouldn't be going to Water-the-loo University?" Several chuckles.

Stan picked up the cup, ready to ram it down a great big hole.

The greasy smile disappeared. "Sorry, pal. I'm being juvenile." Ken pointed at the surrounding chairs with the chewed-off pencil. "Sit down, guys. Looks like our friend is facing some big decisions."

Stan blinked.

"Wanna talk?" Ken held his big hands wide. "We might not have any answers, but we can listen."

Relief washing over him like warm water, Stan smiled. This was no FedEx, but the gang just might do.

So You're Asking the Questions

Concerned about what God wants? Desperate to know what he has lined up for your future? Wishing he would just tell you? If so, you're on the right track. Don't stop asking. Life can take a million directions. Many of them are wrong, taking you places you never wanted to be (Proverbs 14:12).

Wrong Track #1

Many believers at your stage in life don't even ask the questions, let alone find the answers. Some assume their existence is their own, to be spent however they please. They've heeded Satan's whisper: *Do whatever you want. It's your life.*

That's simply not true. The truth is, "He died for all, that those who live should no longer live for themselves but for him who died for them and was raised again" (2 Corinthians 5:15).

Your life is not your own. Not physically, not spiritually. Every breath you take should remind you of the One who keeps those lungs pumping. Every cross you see should bring to mind the Savior who died so your spirit could live. Jesus not only built you, he bought you (Colossians 1:15-16; 1 Corinthians 6:20).

Yes, Christ has dibs on your life. All of it.

Wrong Track #2

Other Christians are aware God has a plan, but Satan has convinced them that life according to God's plan will be boring, miserable, and otherwise undesirable. Another lie. In truth, God's will is *good, pleasing, and perfect* (Romans 12:2). That's what God says. To believe otherwise is to call him a liar.

You want something good? You want to be pleased? You want what's perfect for you? Don't miss it. Discover and live the adventure of God's will for your life.

Wrong Track #3

Many believers have become so frustrated trying to find God's will, they've quit asking the questions. They know it's out there, they assume it's good, but they can't figure out what it is.

Been there?

Here's a sneak peek into the journal of a young lady named Karen, a student in her first year at George Fox University:

God, I'm clueless about what you're doing in my life. I don't know my purpose anymore. I just totally bombed a chemistry test. Are you trying to show me that chemistry isn't for me? I don't get your point right now.

What should my major be? Do you care about my career? Will I ever marry? Who?

God, I'm asking all these questions, yet you seem to respond with silence. I don't understand.

Is that where you're squirming? Not knowing what God wants can get very uncomfortable. No guarantees, but the following principles may relieve some of your discomfort.

Ninety-five percent of God's will is found in the little things. Many believers are fooled into thinking that God only cares about the gorilla-sized issues of life:

- What career should I pursue?
- Whom should I marry?
- Where does he want me to live?
- How many kids should I have—assuming I find a job, get married, and locate a place to live?

That's sad. God doesn't want to share only the big decisions with you; he wants to be a part of the little ones, too. That's why he gave you his Spirit. As the Father's child, you have a built-in Guide to God's will (Romans 8:14).

Learning to be led by that Guide is a lifelong assignment.

As desirable as a FedEx from heaven might seem, Christ prefers dealing with you more personally via his Spirit. This thing between you and Jesus is a relationship, remember? The sooner you learn to hear his still, small voice, the sweeter that relationship will be.

Don't get hung up on whether you should brush with Colgate or Crest tomorrow morning. But do allow yourself to be sensitive to God's Spirit nudging your heart with the things he'd love to have a say in:

- *Your roommate could use a break. Why don't you do her laundry?*
- *Those sunglasses are too expensive. You'd be wiser to go no-name.*
- *See that guy sitting alone? How about eating lunch with him?*
- *Sorry, but that movie will trash your mind. Find something else.*

God's Spirit is trying to communicate with you 24/7. If you hear him on the many little things that compose most of life (Proverbs 3:5-6), you'll find the Spirit's voice easier to recognize when the big decisions make their presence felt (Luke 16:10).

Ninety-five percent of God's will is clearly taught in Scripture. Though God's Word may not say, "Sammy Sutherland should marry Wendy Winterburn," its principles cover the vast majority of the decisions that come your way. And although some portions are admittedly obscure, many of the Bible's directives for your day-to-day existence are absolutely transparent— lights that clearly mark the path God would have you travel (Psalm 119:105).

Consider this verse: "Give thanks in all circumstances, for this is God's will for you in Christ Jesus" (1 Thessalonians 5:18). How much clearer can God get? Thankfulness is his will for you. If you're struggling with not knowing whom you'll marry, this verse translates into something like: "Don't mope. For now, be thankful for the freedom of singlehood."

If you pursue a growing knowledge—and application—of Scripture, you'll find much of God's will is not difficult to interpret.

Ninety-five percent of God's will can be discovered through good counsel. Trying to wrestle out the pros and cons of a big decision on paper? While you're writing, take the time to list a few people you should get input from. Then seek them out. Lay out your options, your interests, your current leanings. Then listen. Listen closely. You may get conflicting counsel. Don't worry about it. One of those people may say something God's Spirit will use, something so crystal clear it drowns out all the other clashing messages. One phrase is often all it takes for God to unveil the door to his will. By looking for help from godly people, you can't go too far wrong. "In the multitude of counselors there is safety" (Proverbs 11:14, KJV).

Ninety-five percent of God's will is accompanied by his peace. Let's begin with the exceptions. Occasionally life on planet Earth will throw decisions at you that are extremely difficult. A situation can be so complex that whatever direction you consider, you'll find doubt and turmoil lurking. Yes, that happens. Find comfort in knowing that Jesus faced history's most heart-rending decision, in a garden called Gethsemane, coming to grips with God's will in the form of a cruel cross. Jesus' turmoil was so great, he sweat blood.

Thankfully, most of life doesn't present such blood-sweating choices.

For all those other, relatively mundane decisions—choices which are still important to both you and God—there is a Spirit-given indicator light that assures you you're on the right track: the peace of God.

When you find yourself worrying about God's will, consider this promise from him:

> The Lord is near. Do not be anxious about anything, but in everything, by prayer and petition, with thanksgiving, present your requests to God. And the peace of God, which transcends all understanding, will guard your hearts and your minds in Christ Jesus.
>
> PHILIPPIANS 4:5-7

As you pray over your decisions, expect God to grant peace when the right option presents itself. Don't move until that peace is yours. Take your time. Not every choice has to be made the instant it comes up. I repeat, not every decision needs immediate attention. God reveals his will at the very best time, no sooner. Sometimes it is God's will for you to be still and wait (Psalm 46:10). Keep praying and seeking until the peace comes.

Peace can help you discern God's will in two ways, by both its coming and its going. If you're enjoying a busy-but-peaceful day, and suddenly that peace disappears, take it as a warning. A red light is flashing in your soul. Stop and reevaluate whatever course you were about to take. Consider the consequences. Find a new direction. Let peace rule again (Colossians 3:15).

Ninety-five percent of God's will is found in the willingness to obey it. Here's an amazing passage on the subject of discerning God's will: "If any of you lacks wisdom, he should ask God, who gives generously to all without finding fault, and it will be given to him" (James 1:5).

God is not stingy in his desire to reveal his will to you. He wants you to know. Really.

But check out the verses that follow: "But when he asks, he must believe and not doubt, because he who doubts is like a wave of the sea, blown and tossed by the wind. That man should not think he will receive anything from the Lord" (James 1:6-7). In other words, if you have any doubts about your willingness to obey God's will once it's presented to you, he will likely remain silent. God is not in the habit of dispensing the knowledge of his will, only to have it thrown back in his face: *Naw, sorry, God. Nice to know your take on things, but I've got a better idea. Thanks anyway.*

Hungry to know God's will? Starving enough to obey it— no matter what? Good for you. You've got the same outlook Jesus had: "My food is to do the will of him who sent me and to finish his work" (John 4:34).

With that attitude burning in your soul, rest easy. You're on the right track. God will make his perfect will clear in good time.

3

Don't Forget to Forgive

*(Dispelling the black mist of bitterness
before you leave home)*

Her stomach churning, Christine was driving too fast. But if
she drove any slower, the bent fender would shake like a nervous diamondback. She pegged the needle on eighty and kept
going. If she went anywhere between sixty-seven and seventy-
three miles per hour, her car would rattle the glasses off her
face. The thought left her head shaking, teeth biting her
upper lip, her eyes stone cold, staring at the road.

Joseph. What a jerk! Why couldn't I have been an only child?

She resisted the urge to stop for coffee. The sooner she
reached Cambridge College, the quicker she could rid herself
of the car she once loved. The fact that a mechanic could fix
it for a few hundred bucks seemed irrelevant. Joseph had con-
taminated her vehicle beyond repair. She would sell it within
a week for whatever she could get.

Doing drugs in my *car? Unbelievable!*

Joseph had done some stupid things in his seventeen years
as her brother, but this beat them all. Now he sat in the county
jail, cooling his heels. Accepting the fact that the incredible
had happened, she strengthened her resolve. Borrowing her
car without permission was borderline forgivable. *This*, however, would not be so easily dismissed. Somehow he'd have to
pay. If his drug habit left him too poor to pay the damages of
last night's fling, she'd get it out of Joseph another way.

Even if it means never talking to him again.

The thought shook her, parting the dark cloud of anger long enough for another thought to slip in: *But if you do not forgive men their sins, your Father will not forgive your sins.*

The car slowed to a dull rattle. Only partly aware, Christine scratched at her neck, trying to decipher the verse's strange meaning. This was bigger than a bent fender—that much was clear.

Judicial Versus Experiential

The verse that rattled Christine's cage (Matthew 6:15) used to confuse me. Did Jesus mean that my salvation was dependent on forgiving others? That sounded scary. I thought my salvation was a *gift* from him, not dependent on any work, even that of forgiveness (Ephesians 2:8-9). So which was true?

My thoughts went in another direction: *Maybe all true Christians are born forgivers; perhaps unforgiveness is not an issue for them.* But that didn't fit with what I knew about myself and had seen in many other believers: Unforgiveness *is* an issue; forgiveness doesn't come naturally. One believer I knew hadn't spoken to her blood brother in over thirty years. Now *that's* sad.

My dilemma was resolved when I made a distinction between *judicial* and *experiential* forgiveness. Allow me to explain.

Judicial Forgiveness
This is what you have in Christ through his death on the cross. God, the righteous Judge, placed your sin on Christ's shoulders, in turn declaring you wholly righteous (2 Corinthians 5:21). You are judged to be completely forgiven—past, present, and future sins included—and that forgiveness is unchanging.

Once forgiven in Christ, you can no longer be condemned (Romans 8:1). That is judicial forgiveness. It knows no measure.

Experiential Forgiveness

Experiential forgiveness is judicial forgiveness that has touched the heart—and in turn touches others (Ephesians 4:32). That kind of forgiveness can be measured. It fluctuates in direct proportion to your spiritual maturity. The more you grow, the greater your experience of God's forgiveness, and the greater your willingness to forgive others.

The converse is also true. If you're not growing spiritually, in all likelihood you're not forgiving, nor are you enjoying God's forgiveness.

The parable of the unmerciful servant is a classic example of judicial forgiveness that didn't touch the heart (Matthew 18:21-35). In this story, a servant—forgiven by his master for a debt he couldn't pay in a hundred lifetimes—turned around and threw a fellow servant in jail for a petty unpaid loan. Though forgiven, the unmerciful servant extended no forgiveness. His shallow appreciation of his own forgiveness left him unwilling to pass that forgiveness on to another.

That's a dangerous place to be.

If you spitefully withhold your forgiveness—the very forgiveness God has so richly granted you through his Son—you'll find God firmly withholding your experience of his heartfelt forgiveness for you. That's what Jesus meant in Matthew 6:15. Instead, like the unmerciful servant, you'll be delivered over to the tortures of guilt, bitterness, anger, vindictiveness, and depression (Matthew 18:34-35). That's a pit of raging dogs that will tear your soul to shreds.

A very painful place to be.

Forgiveness Equals Love

Experiential forgiveness even determines your ability—or lack of it—to love. If you have a miserly estimation of how much God has forgiven you, your love for people will be measured in pennies. But if you spend time meditating on the riches of God's vast forgiveness for your frequently sinful existence, your love for others will know no measure—including your love for people who've hurt you to the core. Instead of wishing God's curse upon them, you'll be praying for their blessing (Matthew 5:44).

Consider Jesus' words as he contrasted the attitude of a repentant streetwalker with that of a self-righteous Pharisee: "Therefore, I tell you, her many sins have been forgiven—for she loved much. But he who has been forgiven little loves little" (Luke 7:47). Your experiential forgiveness determines the measure with which you love people—to say nothing of your love for God. And understand this: You don't need to be a has-been hooker or a three-time murderer to enjoy huge forgiveness. It's all about your depth of appreciation, not about the depth of your sin.

That appreciation only comes through long, humble-hearted meditation.

Without it, you'll be hunted down by the dogs of unforgiveness, no matter how far away your university travels take you. Loving forgiveness is your only escape: *Love ... keeps no record of wrongs* (1 Corinthians 13:4-5).

While packing your bags for college, think about your need for a deep, experiential forgiveness, one that's both felt from heaven and extended to all on earth who've wronged you. Ask God for it. Let him pack your heart full.

Don't leave home without it.

4

On Your Own—But Not Alone

(Antidotes to homesickness)

The mailroom door stood before me, beckoning eerily. It promised delight or disappointment but would not tell me which. I fought the temptation to hold my breath.

Inside the door stood an array of mailboxes, each with its own number and a small glass door. Mine was number 143. Someone had told me those three numbers meant "I love you." To me, they had come to spell "I hate you." My mailbox had been empty for six days running.

As I moved toward that box, my eyes wouldn't focus. Fear held me. One glance through that glass door could reward me with a world of hurt.

Number 143 waited, six inches from my nose. I closed my eyes.

With a homesick heart, it's tough to contemplate the possibility of a mailbox filled with air.

Other than a few weeks of church camp, I'd never left home before. Home was a great place to be. I missed my family and longed for the close comfort of youth group friends. Now I was 959 miles away from them all. Too poor to make a phone call, I would gladly have donated a gallon of blood for a letter from someone—anyone. Even a five-point demerit slip from my Bible college proctor would have brought relief.

With one deep breath, I forced my eyes open. *Empty*.

"I hate you" mocked me in cold silence.

Out of the Pits

I walked through the rest of that day in a numb fog, a zombie to the core. I didn't want to leave; I didn't want to quit. I just wanted to crawl under a rock.

I had a lot of growing up to do, I knew, but knowing didn't take the ache away. One scripture I'd memorized shone a tiny light through my fog: "Cast all your anxiety on him because he cares for you" (1 Peter 5:7). My homesickness was definitely an "anxiety." I should have done it far sooner, but that night I put that verse to the test.

The secluded country road was perfect for what I needed a place to talk, cry, even yell out loud. I did all three. God needed some good reminding of my need for mail. In a dozen different ways, I told him what it was like to have a vacant mailbox. The tears streamed down my face.

Then a thought gently pierced my mind. *Am I not enough?*

I could see my Savior, face sad but smiling, arms open. Love Personified offered me what I needed most. Not a letter, not a phone call, not even a visit from my whole youth group. Jesus offered me more of himself.

I ran into those arms, and that's when the crying really started.

My tears to that point had been bitter, selfish things. They brought zero relief. Now the tears were sweet, cleansing my soul with every drop. I had cast my anxiety on him. In return he showed me his goodness, love, and very real presence. In other words, Jesus hugged my soul.

I gave up begging God for mail. Jesus was more than any letter could be. He filled my mailbox, my world, my very heart.

In reality, he'd always been right with me, ever since I trusted him at age seven. But I needed to grow in order to enjoy his palpable presence. It took the pain of an empty mailbox to begin learning my lesson.

The nearness of Jesus is one of those lifetime courses the Holy Spirit seeks to teach me. I still need to review that lesson each day. As a missionary in Mexico, I occasionally see homesickness raise its ugly head, but it doesn't scare me anymore. My beautiful Savior, Jesus, is right there, every time.

Homesickness Defined

That's part of my story. Let's help you with yours.

Merriam-Webster describes homesickness as the state of "longing for home and family while absent from them." Another writer calls it "a lump in the throat, a sense of wrong." Both are true but not very helpful. You don't want a description of how homesickness feels; you want to alleviate the pain.

It might be more helpful to think of homesickness as an invitation, a summons to step through a Door. It's not the sinister door I imagined the mailroom to have, but a bright one, glowing with the light of a warm fire, filled with promise. No disappointment in that Door, provided you walk through.

Wasn't it Jesus who said, "I am the door"? He went on to say, "If anyone enters through Me, he will be saved, and will go in and out and find pasture" (John 10:9, NASB). Most people limit the great promise of that verse, thinking it merely refers to heaven. True, if you're going to pass through the pearly gates, you'll have to go through Jesus. He's the only Way.

But Christ's salvation is so much more than a free key to glory. You don't have to wait until they build your coffin to enjoy much of what lies beyond that Door. Jesus' salvation is a package deal. It's a house full of presents, a valley of green pastures, a treasure chest of riches to enjoy. And many of those treasures are for here and now. They include:

- Total acceptance in Jesus (Romans 15:7)
- Love unflinching and multidimensional (Ephesians 3:17-19)
- Perfect peace of soul (Philippians 4:7)
- Perfect peace with God (Romans 5:1)
- Full and ongoing forgiveness (Colossians 2:13-14)
- Zero rejection from heaven (Romans 8:1)
- Protection from the evil one (John 17:15)
- And a cure for homesickness from Someone who cares most (1 Peter 5:7)

Feeling homesick? It's a reminder: The Door's open, the fire's lit. Jesus smiles, his arms wide.

Walk on in.

Get Practical, Please

Call it homesickness, loneliness, the blues—whatever—it's all a spiritual malady, a heart problem that needs an internal remedy. You may bury your problem with external things like fun, food, or frenzy, but eventually it will crawl out of its hole, determined to make you sicker than ever.

Thankfully, Christ specializes in internal medicine. When it comes to getting a spiritual diagnosis and finding a cure, Jesus is the Physician to look for.

Following are a few practical suggestions on inviting him in for a house call.

Use Your Imagination

Imagine Jesus alongside as you get up in the morning. See him in the mirror as you brush your hair. Sense his satisfaction as you eat a bowl of cereal. Chat with him as you walk to your next lecture. Allow him to work with you while serving the next customer. Ask him for advice as you polish that term paper. Bid him good-night while you lie down to sleep. Your imagination may be faulty, but the truth stands strong: "Never will I leave you; never will I forsake you" (Hebrews 13:5).

Keep a Journal

Pour your heart out on its pages. Record the thoughts Jesus gives you as you beg him for answers.

Listen to the Loneliness Around You

A sense of utter isolation, even in the midst of a crowd, is a common experience (1 Corinthians 10:13). Make an effort to hear the hearts of others, remembering Jesus was a Master Listener. Ask penetrating questions about the things that haunt people. Realize you're not the only one homesick.

Stretch Your Soul and Reach Out

When you discover the hurts of others, do what you can to heal them. Serve in a soup kitchen for the homeless. Visit residents of a retirement center. As you and Jesus work together encouraging others, you'll be too busy to feel homesick.

Read the Psalms

Many psalms describe the experiences of desperately lonely characters, Jesus included. Consider David's prophetic cry in Psalm 22:6-7, words that describe Christ on the cross: "But I am a worm and not a man, scorned by men and despised by the people. All who see me mock me; they hurl insults, shaking their heads." Loneliness? He's been there.

If all else fails, find a secluded country road, tilt your head toward heaven, and let the tears pour.

He'll be there. You won't be alone.

5

Finding New Friends

(Without having to beg for them)

Tiffany walked through the cafeteria, lunch tray in hand, her eyes wide. She scanned the room, desperate for an empty table. She hated empty tables. But she didn't know anyone, so what choice did she have? *Don't slow down, don't stop, keep moving.* It was all she could do not to swallow. Someone would surely notice such a juvenile gesture, labeling her as a *newbie*— which she *was,* but no sense letting the whole campus know.

This would be a bad time to trip. Oh, she could see it now. Diet Pepsi and BLT launched all over the heads and clothing of three tables' worth of occupants.

The thought made her freeze.

Two guys briefly glanced her way, then casually continued their conversation. Tiffany closed her eyes, unbelieving. *Why am I here in the middle of this walkway acting like road kill? Move!* Opening her eyes, she jerked one foot forward. The tall glass on her tray rattled. Her gaze riveted on the rocking soda, she forced herself forward.

The conversations buzzing around her seemed to pick up a notch. Ears perked, Tiffany heard the word *she* from several directions. Someone else said the word *tray.*

Is every one of them whispering about me? Is there nothing better to talk about? Her eyes, now wider than ever, darted from the BLT to the Pepsi and back. Her breathing grew shallow. Her nose twitched. She needed a place to sit—fast.

Out of the corner of her eye, she saw an empty table.

Go, girl. Total concentration. You can do it. Weaving through scattered chairs, bobbing heads, and table corners, she was within five feet of her target when it happened.

Her toe connected with a chair leg, sending it scraping. Tiffany stumbled forward. *I knew it!* The tray lurched to one side, glass and sandwich plate sliding. Tipping it the other way, she overcorrected. Her lunch seesawed. Tiffany yelped and slammed her tray down with a clatter—two tables beyond the one she had picked.

Heart pounding, head hanging, soda sloshing, she stood, hands like claws on each side of the tray. *Lord, open the ground and swallow me, please.* Unclasping her fingers, her body a bowl of jelly, she folded herself into a chair.

Too embarrassed to look around, she closed her eyes. *Lord, I can't believe that just happened. I'm an absolute wreck! Ever since I've come to this crazy place, it's been a full-time job living inside my head. I think it would help me relax if I had another friend like you, one with skin on. Please send her along soon. Thanks for listening. I know you're there.*

Eyes glistening with tears, she opened them. A blurred figure approached her table. *Great. I'm an emotional basket case, and someone wants to sit with me.* Squeezing the tears away with a blink, she fought to focus.

A beaming face greeted her. "Tiffany?"

Tiffany's eyelids fluttered in confusion. The voice was familiar.

"Do you remember me?"

Tiffany shook her head a quarter of an inch.

"Camp Bethel. I'm Kelly Gibson. We canoed together once."

"You're kidding!" Tiffany broke into a smile. *Wow, that feels strange on my face.* "What happened to all your hair?"

"That's a long story," Kelly replied, one hand rubbing the back of her head. "I can't believe you're here! This place is so huge, I feel totally lost. I was just asking God to help me find someone I recognize."

"Quick, sit down," Tiffany laughed, "before you drop your tray."

Of Leeches, Loners, and Lamenters

Friendship is a strange thing.

You desperately need it. Your soul is designed to thrive on it. You crave for someone to understand who you are and where you've come from. If you don't have it, something aches inside. But when friendship is yours in a deep, unconditional way, your heart sings.

Praise God for Jesus. His unfailing friendship is completely understanding and totally unconditional (Proverbs 18:24).

Yet, when it comes to human friendship, if you cling too tightly, it seems to disappear. People glance at their watches, make lame excuses, are suddenly unavailable. You see them gravitate to others. You grasp, wanting something back, but all you catch is a half-hidden yawn, a roll of the eyeballs, a cold shoulder.

No one likes a *leech.* Someone who sucks people dry, taking with nothing to give.

Soooo. You pull back, you shrivel. You'll never be labeled a leech again. Friendship's not gonna burn you twice.

Instead, you turn into a *loner.* Someone who always prefers to be alone.

Even if you avoid the mistake of being too desperate for a friend, things change. After investing years to make some great relationships, you move, they move. Phones and instant messaging don't quite cut it. It's not over, but it's not the same. You're miles away, facing the challenge of making friends all over again. It's enough to make most people want to cry.

You become a *lamenter*. Someone who moans away the present while dwelling in the past.

Time for a New Outlook

Friendship is not about having. It's about giving.

Think about your forever Friend, the One who sticks closer than a brother. What did you ever do to earn his friendship? Isn't his heart toward you a never-ending flow of unselfish giving? He started your friendship with him by giving his life. He continues to give you his life—all you'll take of it (John 10:10). Give. Give. Give. That's the attitude of the Man who was called a friend of tax-collecting cheats and prostitutes (Luke 7:34). That's the attitude that won your soul to him.

That's the attitude you need to pass on.

If you're a leech, you need to stop leeching. Start giving.

If you're a loner, you need to crack open your shell. Reach out. It's not God's good, perfect, and acceptable will for you to selfishly hide the life he's provided. There are souls—both loners and popular types—whom Jesus wants you to touch. Lose the loner label. Take the risks. Start giving.

If you're a lamenter, crying over yesterday's friendships, you need to get a grip. Splash some cold water on your face. There are people out there more hungry for a good friend than you are—all over the place. Forget about yourself. Go be what they so desperately need. Start giving.

Assuming You're Sold

Ready to take the challenge? Convinced that friendship is something not to be sought but to be imparted? Ready to get beyond merely praying for God to send a friend when his goal for you is so much higher?

Then it's time to take inventory of your abilities as an *amigo.*

Use God's Word to awaken and sharpen the skills you need to deeply bless the people he brings your way. Take a concordance and look under "friend" and its derivatives. Do a study. Meditate large and long on the concept of being a good friend.

Here are a few starting points. Master these and you'll never need to beg God for a friend again:

- A good friend takes interest in the lives of others (Philippians 2:4).
- A good friend listens more than she talks (James 1:19).
- A good friend speaks every word with care (Ephesians 4:29).
- A good friend keeps his promise, even when it costs him (Psalm 15:4).
- A good friend has a handle on destructive emotions (Proverbs 22:24).
- A good friend enjoys being generous, no strings attached (Proverbs 19:6).

- A good friend keeps a confidence, without fail (Proverbs 16:28).
- A good friend knows how to apologize (Matthew 5:23-24).
- A good friend knows how to forgive (Ephesians 4:32).
- A good friend is eager to encourage (Proverbs 27:9).
- A good friend never stops loving (Proverbs 17:17).

Don't Forget

Does it go without saying that Jesus, your best friend, walks with you? Count on it. As you reach out, don't go it alone.

Lock arms with Jesus and be a giving friend.

6

Friends With Fangs

*(Knowing when it's time to shed
the snakes in your life)*

"Pick what you like. I'll get it for you." Jeanette was all smiles.

"I thought you said you didn't have any money."

"Relax, Carmen. I'll get it on credit."

Carmen toyed with an ivory blouse, curious about how well it would go with her new khaki pants. She didn't need to wonder; she knew it would look great. Handing it to her friend, she hesitated. "I don't know if I like the idea of you buying me a gift on *credit.*"

"Oh, don't be such a sissy." With a wink, Jeanette grabbed the top, piled it with several other items, and disappeared into the dressing room.

Ten minutes later she was back. Tossing an armload of clothes into the reject pile, she marched past Carmen. The smiles were gone. "Let's get out of here."

They exited the store before Carmen had the courage to ask, "What did you do with the shirt I picked out?"

"Just keep moving."

"What do you mean?"

"Look, I'm wearing it. Now come on!"

Carmen couldn't see the shirt, but Jeanette's sweater didn't look quite right. They were on the far side of the parking lot before Jeanette slowed down.

"You stole it, didn't you?"

"What does it matter? It's yours. Besides, I didn't steal anything. I've spent all kinds of money in that store. That was just a five-finger discount."

Carmen shook her head in frustration. But that shirt would sure be nice with those pants.

Old as the Bible

The above story has been played out millions of times in real life. It's a plot as ancient as the Old Testament: A good-but-easily-influenced person meets a bad person—and everything goes bad.

"Now Amnon had a friend named Jonadab.... Jonadab was a very shrewd man" (2 Samuel 13:3). In other words, Jonadab was the long-toothed cobra in Amnon's worst nightmare. His sick-minded advice destroyed Amnon's moral purity and deeply hurt Amnon's family. To top it off, Jonadab's friendship cost Amnon his life.

Some friend.

Read the story for yourself (2 Samuel 13). Hopefully, it'll scare you into thinking about the kind of friends you choose. God wants you wide-eyed and sober on this issue. Paul says, "Do not be misled: 'Bad company corrupts good character'" (1 Corinthians 15:33). Translation: Be careful; some of your friends may have fangs.

Assuming you're at least mildly nervous, read on.

Been There, Wish I Hadn't Done That

It was supposed to be a simple walk in the park, a time to goof off. Suddenly the wine bottle showed up. Things were no longer that simple.

"You ever drink this stuff before?"

I was in East Germany. When I arrived, I didn't know a soul. Now I had two friends. I thought I needed them *in the worst way*. Dumb line of reasoning, I know. Before my time there was out, I'd been inebriated three times. I'm talking big time stupidity, vomit all over the place. I was bit by the gotta-have-friends-at-any-cost bug, and the poison sank deep.

It's in the Picking

What are your motives for choosing a friend? Guys tend to ask questions like, "Is he a jock?" "A computer animal?" "Is he funny?" "What kind of car does he drive?" "Can he help me with my homework?" "What's his sister look like?" "Did he actually say 'Hello' without adding 'Geek'?"

Girls may have another set of priorities: "Does she dress right?" "Is she popular?" "Rich?" "Do guys flock around her?" "Am I prettier than she is?"

Those aren't the best reasons for picking someone to hang out with.

You'd be better off with more important criteria, asking questions like, "Is this relationship going to drag me down?" "Is this girl out to use people?" "What's this guy's agenda?" "Will this friendship help me get to know my truest friend, Jesus?" "Is this person open to me talking about my Savior?"

Such questions should make you think twice about your future picks. They may even make you decide to quietly shake certain friends you have now.

This is deadly serious. The kind of people you spend time with will largely determine your life's direction. Your choice may even determine how long you live.

Juan was eighteen, excited about his new relationship with Jesus Christ, anxious to learn more. His desire was to teach God's Word to his native people, the Pima. But he held on to some bad friends. One day those snakes slithered out of the grass, inviting Juan for one last drink—for old time's sake. Juan should have walked away, but he didn't.

Two days later, I dug his grave.

The car had rolled off a narrow mountain road. The driver and Juan's other buddy stumbled away from the accident, leaving Juan to slowly die alone. Some friends.

The Bottom Line

So what is God saying? Don't have any friends unless they pray six hours a day? That's extreme. Even Jesus had a friend with fangs. Remember Judas? Hermit Christians are not what God wants. We're supposed to rub shoulders with those who don't know Jesus. You may be the only way they'll hear the Good News.

"Should I have non-Christian friends?" is not the question. The real questions are, "In this friendship, who's influencing whom?" and, "Is the influence for the good?" If the influence is bad, and your morality is headed south, it's time to peel off some friends. Fast.

Those fangs can hurt.

7

Chewing on God's Word

(When you don't want the Bible to be just another textbook)

"Aaarrrgh!"

Startled, Sarah turned in time to see her roommate heave a booklet across the room. It landed with a clatter in the trash.

"Connie?"

Blowing the bangs out of her eyes, Connie scowled. "I am *sick* of Bible study guides. They're so much like homework, I could puke. Why do I have to 'trace Paul's second missionary journey on the map provided?' The stuffed shirt who wrote that obviously has mistaken me for someone who cares!"

Sarah fought the smile that begged to come. Connie needed understanding right now, not condescension. "Kind of boring sometimes, isn't it?"

"Boring? If only it were that simple. This read-the-Bible-every-day thing is killing me. I've got a course load that could choke an Einstein, and God expects me to stick my schnozzola into this book for three hours every morning like some convent nun in a wimple. I'm sorry!"

"Who ever said anything about three hours?" Sarah hid the escaping smile behind two fingers.

"Whaddaya mean? Every Sunday that preacher you drag me to bangs away on his one-string harp, singing the same lullaby: 'Read that Book. Read it every day!' *Caaaarrrumba!* Every time he preaches, I break into a sweat. The guy is so *intense.*"

The smile disappeared. "I'm sorry you feel like I'm dragging you there. That's the last thing I want for you. We could try someplace else."

"Oh, don't worry about it. It's not the issue. I really do want to study the Bible, but I keep tripping over the fact that so much of it is *obtuse.* I can't understand it. I get to the end of a chapter, and I'm, like, shaking my head, wondering what in Tasmania was that all about?"

Walking over to the trash can, Sarah reached in to retrieve the study guide.

"Leave it there, girl," Connie warned. "I'm done with that thing."

Sarah arched her eyebrows. "What if I want to look at it?"

"Be my guest. Wish you'd taken it far sooner."

"I thought you liked these things."

"Ah, they worked for a while, but I'm done with cramming my brain with more info, coming to the Bible like it's some kind of overgrown textbook." Connie squeezed her stomach. "I've got textbooks coming out of my navel." Grabbing her Bible, she continued, "I want this Book to be rich, tasty soul food, not dry, unspiced turkey stuffing. Am I making any sense?"

Sarah smiled openly this time. "I think I hear you. And I think a single word may help you."

"One single word?" Connie replied. "My, aren't you a paragon of simple solutions."

Sarah nodded, trying to be a paragon of patience.

"Well, what are you waiting for? Hurry. I hope this isn't a *long* word—I've got a class in two hours. Will I need a dictionary? Sorry. I'll shut up. I'm listening. Really."

Sarah paused for five seconds to make sure.

Connie waited, eyes mockingly expectant, mouth clamped shut.

"Meditate."

"Meditate? You're kidding!" Connie's expression turned suspicious. "That's for gurus! Are you trying to turn me into some Eastern mystic?"

Sarah took the Bible from Connie's hands, turning to Psalm 1. Pointing it out, she handed the Bible back. "I've got to go to work. You may want to check out Joshua 1:8 too. We'll talk more later."

Connie flopped herself on the couch—and opened a whole new world.

The One-Stringed Harp

There are many well-meaning people out there with rather awkward approaches to challenging youth to read God's Word. I remember being in Bible college and listening in complete astonishment as one of my classmates screamed at our Romans professor, "I *hate* reading my Bible. My dad *forced* me to read it every morning! He'd spank me black and blue if he found out I hadn't."

That is extreme.

With all the harping on the very real need to study the Scriptures, few Christians do it. Most have tried, but many soon quit. Add the stresses of life on campus, and the number of Bible-reading believers is even scarcer.

That's sad. God really wants you to *like* his Book. He has no desire to see you opening your Bible in grim determination to be a "good Christian." That kind of motivation doesn't last. He wants you to be enthusiastic, not grim, about his Word: "I delight in your commands because I love them" (Psalm 119:47). It's impossible, however, to really enjoy God's Word if you go into it with one of the following attitudes.

"I've gotta do this, or God won't bless me today."
Yowch! What a terrible concept of God—a self-absorbed Scrooge whose two-bit blessings only come if his subjects make him feel good by taking a long look at some ancient manuscript he wrote while in an extra-snarly mood. The real God is no miserly curmudgeon. He longs to abundantly bless you—in fact, he already has. Check out Ephesians 1:3: "Praise be to the God and Father of our Lord Jesus Christ, who *has blessed us* in the heavenly realms with every spiritual blessing in Christ." All you're doing when reading the Bible is discovering how to enjoy that mountain of blessing.

"Let's get this done and get on with life."
It's possible to spend ninety minutes getting zero out of God's Word, the whole time preoccupied with all the "other stuff" that needs attention. I've been there. It's also possible to crack the Bible for five minutes and come away with joyous tears, energized by God to face life's next demand. I've been there, too. It's all in the attitude. It's called *hunger* (Matthew 5:6). If you come to God's Word hungry, you'll leave fed. And it's amazing how nicely that "other stuff" gets done when you give the Scriptures their due priority (Matthew 6:33).

"Five chapters a day keeps the devil away."

Just passing your eyes over onion skin pages isn't the magic wand that makes Satan's knees knock. Consider John's commendation of the youth in his flock: "I write to you, young men, because you are strong, and the word of God *lives* in you, and you have overcome the evil one" (1 John 2:14). God's Word is meant to be a living, breathing entity in your soul. If your appreciation of it stops short of that, you're dead. It'll be the evil one who does the overcoming.

Realize that reading God's Word is not a quantity thing. It's about quality. If it only touches the mind and not the heart, it's *boring*. You're better off reading less and feeding more.

"Time to find out what other heavy-duty commands God has for me to obey."

Choke. If your approach to Scripture is merely a growing list of *do*s and *don't*s, you will gag on that list. I can tell you that from personal experience. My list was so long, I gagged for two years, having lost all desire to study my Bible. Instead I spent a lot of time talking with Jesus, my feet propped up on my desk, hands behind my head. For me it was a time to meaningfully sort out all the Bible truths already crammed into my brain.

When you read your Bible, make it your primary goal to discover more about Jesus: "What's he like?" "How did he handle this?" "How can I enjoy his peace?"

You want to learn about your best friend, the one the *whole* Bible talks about (Luke 24:27). As you grow in your appreciation of all that Jesus is, you'll be far more inclined to ask, *Okay, Lord, what do you want me to do? And how are you going to enable me to do it?*

One Key Word

The word "meditate" really does solve a lot of the frustrations found in people's efforts to appreciate the Scriptures.

First, let's make a distinction between biblical and Eastern meditation. Eastern meditation involves emptying the mind. Satan loves empty heads. He fills them with all kinds of evil ideas and visions. That's dangerous ground. In contrast, biblical meditation occupies your thoughts with God's Word. Satan hates that. A mind dwelling on truth sits in a safe place (Philippians 4:8).

So, what are the advantages of biblical meditation?

Meditation is leisurely (Genesis 24:63).

You can meditate in an easy chair or on your favorite tree stump. No heavy agenda. You sit there and *ruminate.* Think of a cow chewing its cud. It lies completely relaxed, just enjoying the food over and over: *Burp, chew, swallow, burp, chew, swallow.* Excuse the metaphor, but the deep truths of God's Word really do taste better with every swallow.

You can meditate any time of the day (Psalm 1:2).

You don't even need your Bible in hand. You've likely got enough stored in your mind for a hundred meditations. Pick one. Once you discover the sweet experience of meditation, you'll want to read your Bible just so you'll have more to chew on.

Meditation transforms mere knowledge into living truth (Psalm 48:9).
It's one thing to read that God loves you. It's another thing to dwell on the thought long enough that you come away feeling as if your Creator has given you a cosmic embrace.

Meditation comes with a guarantee: God-given success (Joshua 1:8).
True success is not measured or attained by the world's standards. Read Joshua's words for yourself. Then meditate on *that* verse for a while.

God is pleased to see you meditating on his Word (Psalm 19:14). Why? Because as you meditate on his truth, you allow him to express his great love for you. He really wants you to *understand.* Once you understand his heart, you'll in turn love him more. He doesn't want you obeying out of fear; he wants you responding out of love (1 John 4:18-19).

And when you love him more, he is most pleased.

Don't Wait to Start

So kick up your feet. Crack open a Bible. Put your hands behind your head. And make like, well, a contented cow. Ruminate a while.

8

A Sunday Morning Drive

(Guidelines for finding the church you really do need)

You're not even awake when your hand whips out, knocking the shrill alarm clock off its stand. It clatters to the floor. Your heart touches your tonsils.

Did I break it? You slowly shake your head, painfully aware that the clock is almost new. You've been on campus only two months, and money's already kind of tight.

With a poorly stifled groan, you roll over. A rigid arm pushes out from under the sheets, whirling randomly around the floor, in search of the wayward clock. You can't possibly *see* yet, so it takes a while. But you find it because you're getting good at locating things, even with no eyes and one-tenth of a brain.

Rolling onto your back, you hold the clock at arm's length, stretch your eyebrows, and gaze. The numbers are too foggy to read. You depress the LED light switch. The thought registers with the speed of cold molasses: *That won't help in broad daylight.*

Rather than bending your elbow, you lift your head, blinking the bleariness back, trying really hard to see. The effort sends your mind into a swirl. Collapsing back onto the pillow, you squeeze your eyes shut, staring at the shimmering kaleidoscope inside your skull. Your arm falls to your side. Your hand goes limp.

And the clock clatters to the floor.

It's Sunday morning. Time to get excited about going to church.

Do You Need to Be Sold?

One of the first things many Christian students wonder when they're finally on their own is, "Do I need to go to church now?" If you find yourself asking that, it's likely your church experience was a negative one.

Why Not?

The reasons for not wanting to go to church can be complicated, but they may boil down to one or more of the following bones of contention. This book takes a stab—in other chapters—at helping you with these very issues:

- Someone at church did me wrong (chapter three).
- I don't have any friends who'll go to church with me (chapter five).
- Church activities wore me out (chapter eleven).
- My parents dragged me to church every week (chapter fourteen).
- The church is full of hypocrites (chapter fifteen).
- I'm too busy for church (chapter twenty).
- I never get anything out of church. (You may simply need to experience a good church. They're out there. This chapter should help.)

Why Go?

God's desire to see Christians spending time with each other runs deep. He has your best interests at heart: "Let us not give up meeting together, as some are in the habit of doing, but let us encourage one another—and all the more as you see the Day approaching" (Hebrews 10:25).

Did you catch that? The closer we get to Christ's Second Coming—*the Day*—the more we need to be around other Christians. A good church is a great place to find them.

There are two other words in that verse that may sell you on the need for meeting with other Christians: *one another*. Take a computer Bible and do a word search in the New Testament using that short phrase. You'll come up with a list of references that make an interesting meditation. Here's a sample of what you'll find:

- "Serve one another" (Galatians 5:13).
- "Be kind and compassionate to one another" (Ephesians 4:32).
- "Teach and admonish one another" (Colossians 3:16).
- "Encourage one another" (1 Thessalonians 5:11).
- "Spur one another on toward love and good deeds" (Hebrews 10:24).
- "Love one another deeply, from the heart" (1 Peter 1:22).
- "Live in harmony with one another" (1 Peter 3:8).
- "Offer hospitality to one another" (1 Peter 4:9).

You understand that *church* in God's mind is something other than a building and goes way beyond mere meetings. Church is people. Church equals fellow believers. Church means family. You need to go to church to discover the joy of "one-anothering."

You can't get there hiding in your dorm room on a Sunday morning. And the unhappy alternative is a skewed spirit, a shriveled soul, a Christian hermit. Not a good place to be.

So get up and take a Sunday morning drive.

Good Church Ingredients

Your church experience depends much on the quality of the church you attend. You need a good church. While shopping around for a wholesome place to spend a Sunday, consider the following five qualities.

A good church:

Touches Your Spirit

Jesus said, "God is spirit, and his worshipers must worship *in spirit and in truth*" (John 4:24). Some churches, for whatever reason, have no spirit. You walk inside, and icicles hang off the hymnal racks. The Bible may be present, but its presentation fails to stir the soul.

Find a church that challenges you to greater love, worship, and obedience toward God. At the same time, stay away from the extremes. A church that's all "spirit" with no truth is a scary place to be.

Teaches the Scriptures

A solid we-need-to-understand-the-Bible mindset provides the check and balance necessary for true spiritual worship. Without it, religion becomes a wild, emotional roller coaster, with no safety harness and huge gaps in the rails. Any church that does not clearly present the Scriptures as *the authoritative Word of God* will be rife with error. Don't go there.

Provides Solid Mentors

Paul had an intense desire to pass his understanding of walking with Jesus on to the Timothys, Tituses, and Silases of his life. It was a passion he carried right to his last letter, written just before he died (2 Timothy 2:1-2). A good church will have several people with Paul's passion for discipleship. That's a support base you really want to have. If you can't hook up with a good mentor, find a place where you can.

Exercises Your Gifts

As you grow in your relationship with Jesus, your desire to serve him will also grow. Find a church that will utilize the gifts and talents God has given you (2 Timothy 1:6).

Is All About Jesus

Any church that continually speaks in generic terms about "God," with little mention of his Son, is missing the point. Make sure Christ is clearly in the picture. Peter, one of Jesus' best friends, made Christ central: "But grow in the grace and knowledge of our Lord and Savior Jesus Christ" (2 Peter 3:18). If a church doesn't help you know Jesus better, it's the wrong church.

Find a place with all five of the above, and you've got an excellent church. Be there. You don't want to miss it.

When No Church Qualifies

It's possible that your nearest good church is way off in the next province or state. Assuming you've been thorough in your search, and not overly dismissive, you've got a challenge ahead. You have a couple of choices besides just staying home.

Option 1: Settle for a less-than-good church, with the intention of making a difference. Don't be divisive, but do be a blessing. It'll take courage, but God may use you to turn that place around.

Option 2: Start your own cell church right on campus. You'll have to motivate other Christians who are in the same quandary as you. And you'll want to find good leadership. It'll take effort, but the ride could be well worth it.

Do I need to go to church now? The exciting answer is, "Yes!"

9

Jesus With a Jacket
(Finding a mentor worth following)

Two demons paced back and forth, unsure what to do. The big one rubbed his chin, staring at the ground as if trying to burn a trench under his feet. The other waddled like a duckling, glaring at the glow from the nearby dorm room. They stopped as their assigned target opened the window to the evening's breeze, her silhouette dark against the light of her room.

"She's impossible," growled the puny one. "I'm ready to ask for another mission, something less resistant than this saintly slug."

"Fool!" his partner snapped. "Has someone smacked your skull with a pitchfork? Our master would eat us for a midnight snack. We've got to find a way."

"She's tougher to guide than a deaf bat," the little demon insisted. "She won't pay any attention to us. I bet she's studying her Bible right now." He stuck his head through the wall, confirming his suspicion. Then he jumped back, shivering. The Enemy's Book did that to him sometimes.

"We still haven't tried that hunk of a temptation in her World Religions class," he suggested. "He might bring her down."

The two exchanged glances, thrilled by the possibility. Then they shook their heads. Both knew she would tell the "hunk" all about the Enemy, probably resulting in another desertion from their master's ranks. Couldn't have that.

The two demons resumed their pacing. Suddenly the dwarf demon spun on his head, giggling like a jackal. "I've got it!" the imp yelped. He stopped spinning and floated to his feet, savoring the moment.

His partner stared at him as if he'd joined the Enemy. "What are you waiting for? Armageddon? Speak up!"

"Let's tempt her to live the Christian life by herself. We'll separate her from her pastor, her church friends, that Christian professor of hers—we'll convince her she doesn't need them. Let's make her an island, a super-Christian, a loner for God."

"You really do have a brain in that chicken head of yours," the big fiend chuckled. "In three months, maybe six, our target will be so lonely and proud, she'll fall flat on her face. Then we'll have fun with her."

The two demons huddled to plan their attack.

Finding a Mentor

A Couple of Examples to Consider

So you're passionate about your relationship with Christ. You want to serve him with all your heart. Great. Keep going. Make it your life's journey to know and serve him.

But don't do it alone.

Christians who go it solo make a big mistake. Without the support of other believers, you are a prime target for one of Satan's favorite tactics: isolate and conquer. You need the input of other believers in your life, especially that of older Christians.

Contemplate Mary. As a young woman, she found herself miraculously pregnant, the soon-to-be mother of Jesus. Her life was about to undergo major changes. Did she face those changes alone? No. She sought out the counsel and encouragement of her older cousin, Elizabeth (Luke 1:39-56).

Think of Timothy. As a young man he had the smarts to latch on to an older Christian named Paul. Timothy was perhaps twenty-five years younger than Paul was, but he didn't let it scare him. In their long journeys together they saw heathen temples, dark prisons, and many new converts to Christ. Timothy picked up all kinds of great guidance from his coach, ranging from "Don't let anyone look down on you because you are young" (1 Timothy 4:12) to "Endure hardship ... like a good soldier of Jesus Christ" (2 Timothy 2:3).

With the exception of Jesus and his disciples, Paul and Timothy are the closest trainer-trainee team in the whole Bible. Worth imitating, for sure.

So imitate Mary. Be a Timothy. Give yourself protection from Satan and a boost in your desire to live for Jesus. Find an Elizabeth. Search for a Paul. Get yourself a mentor. Fast.

What's a Mentor?
A mentor is a mature Christian person with whom you would willingly share your dreams. A mentor is an encourager, someone whose advice you'd be happy to hear. A mentor is someone committed to seeing you reach your Christ-given potential.

A mentor is someone you would be wise to have in your life.

What to Look for in a Mentor

Availability. Your mentor should be someone willing and able to give you time. If he is always too busy to get together, look for someone else.

A listening ear. Anyone who talks too much won't be much help.

Honesty. You want a mentor who will be brutally honest with you. Sometimes your course in life veers off track. You need someone courageous enough to say so.

Transparency. No mentor is perfect. The ones who can admit their imperfections are worth more than those who hide behind an I've-got-it-all-together smile.

Qualities worthy of respect. Most of all, a mentor should be someone you admire. Make sure you admire her for the right reasons: Just because she's an incredible wakeboarder doesn't mean she has the qualities you need. Look for godly character. Make sure you see Jesus in your mentor's life.

Approaching a Prospective Mentor

It's possible your mentor will come to you. Paul and Timothy were like that. Paul took the first step (Acts 16:1-5). If that happens to you, take the relationship and run with it.

It's more likely you'll have to make the first approach, as Mary did. What you don't want to do is tap Jane Possibility on the shoulder and say, "Hi! Will you be my mentor for life?" You may scare her off.

Instead think about a problem or decision you're facing, something you want help with. Now pick a time and place you'd like to talk about it.

With these in mind, give your prospective mentor a call and say something like, "I've got a problem I need some advice on. Would it be possible for us to get together to discuss it? I'd really appreciate your help on this thing." If she says, "Sure!" (a high probability), suggest your time and place and you're set.

Assuming the first meeting goes greater than you ever expected, try this before you part: "You have been really helpful. Could we do this again sometime?"

There, you've found yourself a mentor. You're now an official "mentoree."

Being a Good Mentoree

Any relationship involves responsibility on both sides. Here are some qualities you'll want to have:

Be punctual. Most mentors are busy people. Don't waste her time by being late or failing to show.

Be outgoing. Don't wait for your mentor to initiate the conversation. Come up with discussion topics before you get together. Let your mentor know what it is you expect in the relationship with him.

Be open. You need to start out carefully, but you want to be able to eventually share the bottom line in your life—your biggest pain, your deepest struggle. You can't get help for things you hide. Once a firm bridge has been built in the relationship, it's unlikely you'll shock your mentor with anything you've done or experienced. He's probably done or experienced something similar.

Be considerate. Make sure the relationship with your mentor doesn't eclipse your growing friendship with Christ. If you let that happen, you'll become a leech who monopolizes your mentor's time. She should willingly give you time, but she has her own life to live, too. Discover the healthy balance.

Be hungry. Ask questions—lots of them. Write down the answers. Tell your mentor if his or her advice helps. If it doesn't, gently let him know and invite more input. Watch your mentor— see what makes him tick. Find out how he and Jesus relate.

Most of all, be relaxed. You're not going to solve all your problems in one sitting. Make sure you do both serious and fun things. It's amazing how much you can learn playing tennis or chopping wood together.

A Few Other Suggestions

Guys need male mentors. Girls need female mentors. Cross the gender gap and you're asking for trouble. Dangerous attractions have a way of complicating things.

Realize God may have several mentors for you during the course of your life. Don't feel locked into having only one. People move. Relationships change. Avail yourself of as many mentors as you reasonably can. Each will help you in different ways, at different times.

Understand the ultimate goal of mentoring: Mentorees are meant to become mentors themselves. Just before Paul died, he wrote Timothy these words: "And the things you have heard me say ... entrust them to reliable men who will also be qualified to teach others" (2 Timothy 2:2). The Christian life is meant to be a transformation from being a Timothy to being a Paul. Learn well the role of Timothy. With time you'll become a Paul.

One word of caution: There's a chance your relationship with a mentor will become destructive rather than helpful. If a mentor begins to control your life, becomes unduly critical, or suggests something you know is a violation of God's Word, get out of the relationship. It's a slim possibility. Be forewarned, but don't let the potential of one bad apple spoil the full barrel of good mentors that are out there.

The Bottom Line

It's simply this: *Don't be a loner for God.* Instead, look for the mentors God has lined up for you. No sense slashing your way through life's problems by yourself. There are good people around who'll gladly help cut the trail.

Imitate Mary. Elizabeth's waiting.

Be a Timothy. Find your Paul.

10

Go for the Gold
(Choosing a worthwhile purpose in life)

A trickle of sweat creeps into his eye. The Olympic marathon runner pushes forward in spite of the sting, the long strides of his remaining opponent a blur of motion ahead. Twenty-three miles already lie behind them.

The real pain begins.

Gauging each desperate breath, he runs a shade faster. His left calf threatens to cramp. He ignores it and gazes at his opponent's number—129. *Beat that guy and the gold is yours*, he reminds himself. The number becomes a robotic chant in his foggy mind, each step a digit: *1...2...9...1...2...9...*

The chant spurs him forward. His pace quickens. With patient determination, he draws even with, then passes his opponent. Number 129 grunts, angry at losing first place.

Olympic Stadium hovers nearer with each step, its entryway a dark, beckoning hole. Lungs rasping, the marathoner strains to stretch his stride. His legs eat up the distance. A shadow cools his head for an instant, and then he bursts through the entryway into the stadium. The chatter of forty thousand spectators subsides. An oval track lies ahead. Four hundred meters to go. The gold awaits him.

Suddenly, his left calf locks in racking pain. Stumbling, he fights to stay on his feet. Pounding shoes buzz by him. Regaining his balance, he stares in dismay.

The number 129 stares back.

Teeth gritted, eyes burning, arms pumping, he runs after

the number, his mind screaming the digits—*One! Two! Nine! One! Two! Nine!* Leg threatening to explode, he bites back the agony. At this point in the race he would rather die than miss the gold.

Life's Big Question

If you haven't asked the believer's huge question of life already, now's a good time. The question may come in various disguises, but when stripped to the bone, it looks the same each time:

What is the purpose of my existence?
What will bring the most satisfaction out of life?
Is there something beyond sleeping, eating, working, studying, and playing sports?

As different as those three questions may seem, they all have the same answer. They're summed up in the following question: "Why did God save me?"

Many believers are foggy on the answer to that question. As a result they spend their days doing one of two things: Chasing vacuous dreams God never gave them or living mediocre lives that know no dream.

You don't want to go down either of those two unhappy trails. You want to have a crystal clear understanding of why Jesus has kept you on this planet when both he and you know that you would be far happier with him in heaven.

So ask him again: *God, you want me here for a reason. What is it?*

The answer to that question can also be considered from several sides, but as with the facets of a diamond, no matter how many sides you gaze at, the gem is still the same at the core. Gaze here at some of the facets for your purpose in life, your God-given reason for being:

To make God shine by living a fruitful Christian life (John 15:1-8)

To discover and live out the adventure of God's good, perfect, and acceptable will (Romans 12:1-2)

To love God with everything that's in you (Mark 12:30)

To know Jesus in every way there is to know him (Philippians 3:10)

To be Jesus' friend, willingly doing whatever he asks of you (John 15:14)

Which of those facets most appeals to you? I like them all, but the life purpose that really speaks to me is this: When I stand before my eternal Judge, I want to win the prize (2 Timothy 4:7-8). Like that Olympic marathoner, I'm in a race. And without a doubt, I want to finish it. I'm going for the gold.

Does that sound selfish? Greedy even? I don't think so.

This Missionary's Marathon

I run my race as a missionary to the Pima Indians of northwestern Mexico. My race has had its bright moments, but at times it's also been painful.

I've been slandered, ridiculed, growled at, and ignored. They've stolen my water line, vandalized my truck, and trashed my house. Twice my life has been threatened, once I've been shot at. The town I live in is like the Wild West, only now the cowboys and Indians use machine guns. I've shaken hands with eleven known killers and buried more friends than I want to count.

I sometimes ask myself the big-purpose-in-life question: *Why do I put up with this thankless grief?* All I've ever done is given them medicine for their bodies and God's Word for their souls.

Why? It's simple: At this point in the race, I'd rather die than miss the gold.

Better Than Olympic Gold

The day you trusted Christ, you, too, entered a lifelong marathon (Hebrews 12:1). Jesus offers prizes to each runner, not for winning but for finishing the race (2 Timothy 4:7). The prizes consist of gold, silver, and precious stones (1 Corinthians 3:12). Leading runners even win crowns (1 Peter 5:1-4). And unlike Olympic medals, Christ's rewards will last forever (1 Corinthians 9:25).

Eternal rewards are worth running for.

But how does a Christian run the race well? By serving God with enthusiasm, like a wholehearted runner (Colossians 3:23). By using every single day wisely, conscious that time is ticking by (Ephesians 5:16). By unflinchingly suffering with Jesus, knowing that running sometimes involves pain (Romans 8:17-18). And by not quitting in the middle of the race, confident that Jesus runs alongside (Hebrews 12:1-3).

Christ will greet every winner at the finish line with the

words "Well done, good and faithful servant!" (Matthew 25:21). Hearing those words is a purpose worth striving for—more precious than any Olympic gold.

Lacking a worthy purpose in life? It's not because there's none out there.

Fill It Full

Here's a slightly different way of looking at life's purpose: Imagine yourself with a large bag. You're aware that every kind word, every friendly smile, and every cup of cold water has a reward if done with the attitude of serving Jesus (Mark 9:41). Your assignment from God is to live in such a way that Jesus can fill that bag with gold, silver, emeralds, rubies, diamonds, and crowns.

You want that sack crammed full.

So you volunteer to cut your elderly neighbor's lawn. As the grass flies, you're praying, *This is for you, Jesus.* The smile on your face is three yards wide. *Keep filling that sack for me, Lord. What do you figure this job's worth, anyway? A couple of silvers?*

Then you start seeing opportunities everywhere: a pile of dishes, a poor family with no Christmas, a summer missions trip, a classmate's need to hear about Jesus. You eagerly jump in at each opportunity, owning Jesus as your guide, your motivation. Meanwhile, the gold, silver, and precious stones keep pouring in. You want that bag to burst with rewards.

But doesn't that seem a little selfish? Greedy even? Not if you're excited about someday seeing Jesus. Read on.

Exhilaration Versus Embarrassment

Let's assume you've filled that bag. Your race finished, you are now presented before the King of kings. Having discovered the believer's great purpose, having served your Savior without reserve, you walk toward him. Your heavy sack bends you low, but your smiling face shows no strain.

As you approach the throne, you fall to one knee. And with the twenty-four elders who've gone before you, your soul bursting with unspeakable joy, you spill your rewards at Jesus' feet (Revelation 4:10-11). *Here you go, Lord. This is all for you. You sure deserve it. Every bit.*

There's nothing selfish or greedy in that. Zilch.

But hear this loud and clear: When that day comes, some believers will be holding an empty bag (1 Corinthians 3:10-15). You don't want to be one of them.

Hi, Jesus. Thanks for saving me. That was great. I'm real thankful to be here and not in that other place. By the way, sorry I didn't finish that race you gave me. I never even really started. Silly of me, I know. Look at this empty sack I'm carrying. Kind of a shame, isn't it?

Ouch. Gag. Squirm. For a believer there could be nothing more painful, gut-wrenching, or embarrassing than that.

Understand, this isn't about heaven or hell. Christ settled that huge question for you with his blood. This is about eternal rewards—or the absence of them—depending on how fully you live out the answer to life's other big question, *Why did God save me?*

So run your race. Fill that bag. Pour the life Christ has given you into serving him. He'll pay big-time and long-term on your investment.

Go for the gold.

11

No Sweat
(Getting out of the heat of frenzied ministry)

I nearly killed myself trying to serve Jesus.

I was sixteen, a follower of Christ, and enthusiastic about it. I read my Bible, prayed, and spread the gospel to everyone who would listen. Our church youth group was on fire for Jesus, and I was one of the handful who got it there. Every time those church doors opened, I ran inside. I taught Bible studies, did door-to-door witnessing, edited a newsletter, set up chairs before meetings, took them down after, and earned the highest award in Christian Service Brigade (read: a guys-only AWANA program or a Christian Boy Scout troop).

Talk about busy for God.

During those days I got more phone calls than the rest of my family combined. "It's for you, Manfred," Mom would say, eyes still riveted to her book. I had big people to see, important things to discuss, hot sermons to preach.

My schedule looked like a turkey with too much stuffing:

- **Monday:** No church. Get some homework done.
- **Tuesday:** Visitation night for youth. Door-to-door evangelism.
- **Wednesday:** Christian Service Brigade. After-meeting leadership huddle.
- **Thursday:** Youth night. After-meeting social.
- **Friday:** Bible study for "on-fire youth." Edit the teen Sunday school newsletter.

- **Saturday**: Youth outreach event. Bring a friend, and see him trust Jesus.
- **Sunday**: Sunday school (pass out those newsletters). Morning service (help in children's church). Youth football game (tackle). Evening service (sometimes preach). Another after-meeting social (restaurant: cheap, nice atmosphere, desserts only).

I did all that for a grueling year and a half.

At eighteen I was burnt out. I slashed my schedule and even skipped many of the things I really wanted to attend. For three months I slept thirteen hours a day. Like a bear just out of hibernation, I was still tired when I woke up. This all-out-for-God thing had lost its glitter. I was depressed and secretly hoping to die.

Like I said, I nearly killed myself trying to serve Jesus.

Unfortunately, I didn't learn my lesson. After my junior year at New Brunswick Bible Institute, I took on the *huge* responsibility of being program director for a family camp that at its peak hosted one thousand-plus people. By the end of that summer I was so emotionally and physically exhausted, I had no desire to go back to Bible school. My mind and soul had been thoroughly fried.

A Note to Anyone Who Hasn't Been There

Some Christian youth need a loud wake-up call to get out and serve their Savior. He has given every believer the tools to do so (1 Peter 4:10). That includes you. You need to learn to use those tools, the gifts and talents God would have you utilize for the rest of your life to glorify him (2 Timothy 1:6). Moreover, you have been "created in Christ Jesus to do good works, which God prepared in advance for us to do" (Ephesians 2:10). Good works didn't save you (Ephesians 2:8-9), but they are part of the package deal that comes with knowing Jesus.

Mark this well: God's great program for this poor world has no room for laziness.

Good News for "Been-There-Done-Thats"

But some of you, like myself, need to hear a different message: God doesn't want you to sweat to death serving him.

Ezekiel, one of God's prophets, gave some clear instructions to the Jewish priests of his day. He wrote, "They are to wear linen turbans on their heads and linen undergarments around their waists. They must not wear anything that makes them perspire" (Ezekiel 44:18).

God didn't want his ministers to sweat, period. He still doesn't.

We're talking figuratively here, now. If your service for God is getting harder to face, becoming an empty grind, pushing you toward burnout, you're working on your own steam. You're sweating. Jesus doesn't need your sweat. It stinks to high heaven.

What *does* he want? Mostly Jesus wants you to enjoy his love (Ephesians 3:16-19). He wants you to be filled with peace (Colossians 3:15). He wants you to find rest (Matthew 11:29-30). All three of those—love, peace, and rest—are guaranteed antiperspirants for the sweating child of God. Think about it: A guy in love with a nice girl avoids the offensive smell of sweat. (That probably works both ways.) And a guy full of peace and rest isn't working so hard that his soul perspires.

Concentrate on Christ's love, peace, and rest, and you'll find a growing power working within (Ephesians 3:7,20). That power will enable you to serve God in a way that will far outdistance your feeble efforts. And it's a power that won't leave you panting on the side of the road, thinking about dying.

No sweat. That's where God wants to take you.

One Major Disclaimer

We're not talking about literal sweat here. We're talking figurative sweat in the spiritual realm of your life, remember?

So if you're a runner, go ahead and work up a lather running the fastest mile you've ever run. If you're digging a ditch, set the pace and work so hard you're the first one to drip. That kind of sweat is great. God definitely desires for you to be wholehearted in all you do (Colossians 3:23).

Use Your Nose

Learn to recognize the stink of sweat in your service for God: a heart that groans at the sight of a church; emotions that balk at the thought of doing anything else for Christ; a mind that questions, *Does God even pay attention to all my hard work?*

Those are all signs of a sweating soul.

Don't keep perspiring until you flop from spiritual heatstroke, as I did. When the reek of spiritual sweat reaches your nostrils, bathe yourself in the basics: God's love for you, his desire for your peace, and the relaxing rest that comes in

Christ. Enjoy them. Saturate yourself in them.

And stay there until you stop sweating.

Then, renewed and refreshed, you'll be able to serve God again. In his strength, not your own.

12

Wrong Risks, Right Risks
(Living dangerously for all the right reasons)

My youth group was having a scavenger hunt, and we had a list of junk to bring back to the church, everything from *teddy bear* to *lawnmower*. Anyone with a vehicle became a team captain. First team to finish the list won.

I was a captain.

And I had a Camaro. Wide tires and a hot 305 under the hood. Five of us crammed into my car and took off. Fishtailing through the gravel, I nearly sideswiped a van. I got around it, who cares how. Now everyone could suck our dust.

We rocketed to my place, loaded up, and scrambled back, lawnmower sticking out of the trunk like a half-closed jack-knife. Using a back road, I hit ninety MPH, trashing the limit by fifty, looking to see if my teammates were scared. It seemed like great fun.

Then came the stoplight. We were a quarter mile away when it turned yellow. I didn't touch the brake. We'd wasted too much time at my place. We needed to make this light. Too bad I had to make a left turn.

The light turned red half an hour before we reached it.

I stomped on the gas, then hit the brakes and cranked the steering wheel. My tires, screeching in protest, fought to grab the asphalt. But cars don't do lefties while speeding. I pushed the brake to the floor.

A flush of panic attacked me. A lamppost rushed for the passenger door. This beautiful car was about to wreck. Worse still, some of us would get hurt.

Great fun? Not even.

Two wheels tapped the curb and it was over. We drove on to our church, laughing nervously, arriving in second-to-last place.

Coming to My Senses: Why Did I Do That?

Wrong risk. Stupid risk. A risk I'm embarrassed I took.

As guys we want to flex our muscles, make our mark, show the world we exist. But we sure pick weird and dangerous ways to go about it sometimes. There's a football player from my hometown who now lives in a wheelchair. On a dare he tried to smash open a steel door—helmet first. Experimenting with drugs at the time didn't help.

I hurt for him—and wonder why I didn't end up like him.

But wrong risks aren't only a guy problem. A museum once had a loaded shotgun on display, pointed at the viewer, set to fire sometime in the future. People lined up by the hundreds for the cheap thrill of smiling at death.

Then there's the whole dark world of initiation rites: new members closed up in a coffin for unknown lengths of time, or forced to strip while being beaten with whips. (This happens in both fraternities *and* sororities.) One initiate was blindfolded, then tied to a set of train tracks. When the train came, he had no idea he was on an unused side rail. He died of a heart attack while the train passed by. I think they made him a posthumous member. Great.

Not every fraternity or sorority is evil, but many—better still, most—are. As a Christian, enter with great caution.

Whether it's an extreme sport that's gone too extreme or

an invitation to trash the dorm on Halloween night, wrong risks are never as rewarding as they appear at first glance. More often than not, they're painful. Proverbs says, "Penalties are prepared for mockers, and beatings for the backs of fools" (19:29). And even if you don't pay the earthly consequences, like a broken leg or experiencing the inside of a police car, you earn yourself a blemished conscience before God.

It's not worth the risk.

Right Risks: God's Glory Is the Goal

If you do something wild just for the head rush, you need to wonder if God is in it. He didn't give us life to waste it on self-ish thrills. But God *does* want our lives to be exciting. He delights in seeing his children be bold and fearless for him.

Like Stephen, stoned for his faith, praying for his enemies' forgiveness, too bold to keep silent. He took a risk, told those who hated Jesus they were wrong—and died for his stand. Jesus was so thrilled by this display of holy bravery, he was standing, arms open wide, ready to receive Stephen's soul when it finally left this cruel planet (Acts 7:54-60).

Then there's Dorr Granger, my missionary partner. One night he was returning to his University of Michigan dorm after leading a Bible study. Suddenly a half dozen gorillas from the U of M football team jumped from a second story balcony and surrounded him.

"Hey, Granger, you too good for us? How come you don't party with us anymore?"

These guys were a little high and very agitated. Dorr had a choice: start partying or get praying. He prayed. And while he prayed, he told them about Jesus, the friend who made life better than any party he'd ever been to. When he finished, the gorillas nodded, stood aside, and let Dorr go home untouched.

"That guy's got a cool head, man."

Of all the scary things you could do, telling people about Jesus Christ is definitely a risk, but a high and noble one. Go for it. When you first start, you may say dumb things and make mistakes. That's okay. God sees your heart. With time he'll mix wisdom with your boldness.

And you'll talk about your Savior more than ever.

A Risk I'm Glad I Took: Wonderfully Wild

I stopped to help a truckful of men with a slow leak in their tire. They needed a pump, and I had one. With the pump puttering away, I noticed the bed of their truck was piled with empty beer cans.

I picked one up. I still can't believe what came out of my mouth.

"See this, guys?" I began, holding the can in the air. "God's Word teaches that all drunks will face punishment in a horrible place called hell." Ouch. Did I say that?

I went on. "And I'm no better. I'm as much a sinner as any of you." I shared with them a little of my own foolish adventures in alcohol. Heads nodded, mixed with smiles.

I went on to tell them about the One who loved them— loved them to death.

They still like their beer. But Mike has asked me for a Bible. And Ray would like to hear more.

Sharing Jesus is a risk that never grows old, never loses its thrill.

It's a risk worth taking.

13

Each Stick Had a Name

*(Missions: A career choice Jesus himself
wants you to consider)*

Dave Wall steps off the bush plane into the plush green scene
before him. It's like working for *National Geographic.* The first
thing that hits him is the fetid heat. Gasp. Whatever the
jungles of Papua New Guinea smell like, this must be it.

Bugs the size of golf balls buzz by his ears, noisy as the plane
he just crawled out of. And the humidity hangs thick. Dave, a
hockey hopeful from Alberta, Canada, has never sweat like
this before. Might as well be walking through a sauna.

Suddenly a dark-skinned mob surrounds the plane, jumping like popcorn in a hot, lidless pan. Unfamiliar shouts fill
Dave's ears. The language—if you can call it that—sounds like
a bad cough and a mouthful of marbles.

These people are so excited!

They call themselves the Bisorio. They're convinced some
more missionaries have come to live in their tribe. They've just
heard the gospel, the story of Jesus, and it's the best news
they've ever heard. They're not afraid of the "forever fire" anymore. These people are grateful for the missionaries among
them, Dave can tell.

But Dave doesn't want to be a missionary. He's only a short-
timer here. He has lived all his life in the shadow of Prairie
Bible Institute, a college that sends missionaries all over the
world. It may be okay for outsiders to come to PBI and think
about missions, but if you've grown up there, it's definitely not
cool to want to be a missionary.

Professional hockey—now, that's cool. And if it doesn't work out, Canada's Royal Canadian Mounted Police is the way Dave will go. Colorado Avalanche—maybe. The Mounties—a definite possibility. Missions—not a chance.

But here he stands, staring at the people missionaries have come to work with, eyeballing the job missionaries do, considering the missionary calling God is slowly injecting into his soul. Wow.

Dave shakes his head. He's not convinced.

He walks to the missionaries' jungle home, gym bag in hand. Jabbering children dance alongside. He wonders if this short-term missions thing is a mistake.

The first day turns to evening. Suddenly, startling news runs through the Bisorio village like a pack of wild pigs. A delegation of five men from a neighboring tribe has come to visit. They call themselves the Malaumanda. They want a "big talk" with the missionaries. Now.

Dave finds himself sitting in the meeting. The light of a campfire flickers on dark, glowing faces. He hopes these Malaumanda don't mistake him for a real missionary. After two weeks he's out of here. Real missionaries stick around for a long time.

Dave rubs his nose on the sly. Wow, do these guys smell strong.

Gleamase, the oldest man, speaks up for his fellow Malaumanda: "We want a missionary like the Bisorio have. We're afraid of the forever fire. We don't want to die without hearing the message the Bisorio have heard. Send us a missionary. We will take him home with us. Tomorrow."

The missionary translates the message into English. Then silence hangs in the air. Dave looks at his fellow short-termers.

Everyone's eyes are wide. Dave swallows thickly.

The missionary to the Bisorio responds, "We would love to send someone to the Malaumanda, but no one is available right now."

Gleamase frowns. He translates the message into his native tongue—another mouthful of marbles. His tribesmen get agitated as they listen.

"What do you mean, you have no missionaries?" Gleamase demands. "What about you?" Gleamase's finger points right at Dave. "You come with us. Tomorrow. We need a missionary. Now."

Dave stares at the pointed finger, his heart rattling like a machine gun. His eyes beg the missionary host for help.

"These people can't be missionaries yet," the missionary says, his voice faltering. "They need more education so they can learn your language. And people from their home country must send them, helping so they can afford food while they live among you. None of these people can come to you for at least another two or three years."

Dave's heart sinks. The explanation is reasonable, but it still sounds lame. He can feel God pouring something into his soul, something Dave isn't sure he wants to have.

Back in Canada Dave had his eye on a girl named Cindy Allen. Cindy Allen is very *fine*. Cindy also knows without a doubt that she wants to be a missionary. She isn't interested in guys who aren't thinking missions—Dave included.

Now Dave has a dilemma. If he lets this Gleamase guy talk him into being a missionary, it will seem bogus back home. "Hi, Cindy, I finally decided I should be a missionary. Wanna marry me now?" Yeah, right.

The days disappear in waves of heat, noise, and smell. Dave works, building a missionary home in the hazy sun. After each day's work is done, he quietly observes.

One afternoon he watches several Bisorio believers get baptized. His brothers and sisters in Jesus, he realizes. Family. With New Guinea as a memory, Canada will never be the same. Dave's world has expanded.

Days later Gleamase and gang continue to hang around the Bisorio village, refusing to return to their own. They're still hunting for missionaries.

Dave is determined not to get caught. One more day and he's gone.

He and the missionary are walking together when Gleamase and his groupies show up. Gleamase gets in the missionary's face, insisting they sit down. Now. He has something to say.

Dave sits on the airstrip grass, where tomorrow an airplane will take him away. He finds himself facing the Malaumanda spokesman. Gleamase could touch his nose from where they sit.

But Gleamase touches something far deeper.

In his hand is a bundle of small sticks. He picks one out and holds it in the air. "This stick is Wadu. He sits beside me right now. You have decided not to send us a missionary. That means Wadu will fall into the forever fire." With a snap of the wrist, Gleamase throws the stick to the ground.

The stick lands before Dave's crossed legs.

"This stick is Wayama. She is back in our village. She is old. She is very afraid of the forever fire. But that's where Wayama will go if you do not send us a missionary." The stick falls, resting across the first.

Head hanging, Dave stares.

"This stick is Bani. He is only a little child, but that doesn't matter. If you don't send us a missionary, the forever fire will swallow him. We all die someday." Another stick flips through the air, bouncing against Dave's big toe.

Dave Wall is no crybaby. He's a hard-hitting hockey player. But as the sticks fall in a pile at his feet, the tears pour. And the sticks keep coming, each with a name.

With a small rustle, the last stick joins the others. Then silence rules.

Suddenly, tugging the missionary by his shirt-sleeve, Dave blubbers, "Tell him that I can't come to his village right now." He then grabs the pile lying before him: "But make sure he understands that I'll talk to everyone I can about his people. I'll show them these sticks. I'll tell them the names they possess. And someday, hopefully soon, some of them will come."

The missionary translates while Gleamase stares into Dave's glistening eyes. When the translation is done, he nods but does not smile. It's not enough.

Dave tugs the missionary's shirt again, desperate. "Make sure he knows I'll be coming. As soon as I possibly can, I'll be here as a missionary. Tell him. Now."

Gleamase nods as he listens, his face still stern. Dave needs no translator for the expression he sees: "Get going, young man. Find us a missionary. Be one yourself. And hurry—I won't be here forever."

The Epilogue

Two thousand years ago Jesus told his disciples, "The harvest is plentiful, but the workers are few. Ask the Lord of the harvest, therefore, to send out workers into his harvest field" (Luke 10:2).

Today Dave and Cindy are missionaries in Papua New Guinea. With them are their five children. They've shared Jesus with the Pukapuki people, neighbors to the Malaumanda.

The Malaumanda also have their own missionaries now. Sixty of them know Jesus as their Savior, and they're studying the Book of Romans in their native tongue, no longer afraid of the forever fire. God has their names written in heaven, including Wadu's.

But things happened too slowly for Gleamase. He was murdered before a missionary could tell him the Good News.

There's no time to wait. People need Jesus.

Does God want you to be a missionary? A short-term missions trip may be the best way to find out. Go for it.

In the meantime, ask the Lord of the harvest to send more missionaries. Now.

Thanks.

14

So Your Parents Aren't Perfect
(How to honor them anyway)

"Why do you even bother, Dad?"

"I always hold doors open for a lady. Just trying to be a gentleman."

"That is so ancestral."

"You calling me old again? That kind of hurts."

"Sorry, Dad, but why can't you be like everyone else and just walk through the door?"

"Simply because I still need to do what I think is right. It makes me who I am."

"You ever think of *changing* who you are into something more respectable?"

"Wow. I'm not sure you understand the meaning of the word."

"Whatever."

Two Verses That Carry a Big Stick

"'Honor your father and mother'—which is the first commandment with a promise—'that it may go well with you and that you may enjoy long life on the earth'" (Ephesians 6:2-3). I know this is bad, but I've always had trouble taking that passage at face value. It strikes me as a bit too simplistic, too all-encompassing. Does it mean that everyone who is nice to their mom and dad will live past one hundred? And what about the that-it-may-go-well-with-you part? Is God saying that if I'm respectful whenever my parents show up, life won't have any major problems?

Maybe. Maybe that's *exactly* what God means—or something close. This *is* God's Word we're considering here. No matter how much our finite minds wrestle with Scripture's real implications, we cannot dismiss it as *not true* (John 17:17).

It's easy to think of situations where a guy rejected everything his parents stood for, then suddenly died in a tangled mess or faded away with AIDS. That kind of story makes simple sense of the promise: "Honor ... that it may go well with you." It's clear that if you dishonor your parents, life will be rough and may be short.

But what about all those godly, parent-honoring teens who die a young death, their bodies destroyed by leukemia? It happens, and the reasons why aren't simple.

It may help to realize there are other verses equally as true as the words "that you may enjoy long life." Try this one on for size: "Precious in the sight of the Lord is the death of his saints" (Psalm 116:15). Occasionally it seems that heaven decides a parent-honoring teen should leave this cruel world and come home—where he and God can enjoy each other face-to-face. God is sovereign. God is neither mean nor selfish, but he can do what he wants.

One thing is for sure: This job of honoring Mom and Dad doesn't go away when they drop you off at the campus dorm. Nor are you exempt from this command because you've suddenly discovered that the dad you once thought was kind-of-quirky-but-mostly-cool is really *far* from perfect.

Don't get it wrong: This command is for you. And remember, we could be talking life or death here. This passage of Scripture has clout.

Convinced? Eager for a chance at long life? Hungry to be free of the struggles that come with a can't-stand-my-parents heart? Here are a few practical suggestions on what honoring your parents should look like.

Love them where they're at, not where you want them to be (1 Corinthians 13:1-8).

It's easy to find fault in your parents' lives. Any Bible-toting Pharisee can do that. True maturity loves people in spite of their faults. Your greatest test of maturity may lie in loving your parents *for who they are*, not holding out on them because they haven't reached your idealistic image of what they should be. Learn true love at the feet of Jesus. Then pass that love on to your parents.

Pray for them often (1 Timothy 2:1).

Your respect for your parents—or lack of it—is directly reflected in how much you pray for them. Pray little, respect less. Pray much, honor lots. Every time you sincerely bring them before God, seeking their best, something good in your heart grows.

Take an interest in their lives (Philippians 2:4).

Growing up, you probably never broke a sweat getting to know what makes your parents tick. If you're like I was, the main concern was to avoid ticking them off. That needs to change. You're an adult now. To whatever level they allow you, ask your folks penetrating questions in an effort to know them. Feel their heartbeat. Take an interest in them as *people*. Your respect for them—and theirs for you—will blossom.

Assume they've learned a few things about life (Proverbs 13:1).
Okay, so you've made the valid observation that your parents
don't know everything. Good. But don't jump to the conclusion that they don't know squat. If they've raised you for eighteen years without bouncing off rubber walls, they've probably
learned a thing or two. Glean from their insights. You don't
have to buy everything they say, but at least give it fair consid-
eration. God may actually want to tell you something through
them. And if God's speaking, you don't want to miss it.

**Don't just trash any conservative value they've tried to pass on
to you (Proverbs 6:20).**
If your parents consider themselves "frugal," making a dollar
stretch three miles will be important to them. You may view
them as outright tightwads. Hmmm. Show some restraint in
your thinking. They may be a tad extreme—cutting coupons
out of twelve newspapers—but you'd be most unwise to completely dismiss the value that hides behind the extreme. So
don't scoff at a ten-dollars-off coupon. Use it. Capture the spirit
of what your parents have sought to teach you, even if you
can't carry it out to the letter.

**Be careful that your attempt at advice doesn't become a curse
(Proverbs 20:20).**
Your well-intentioned efforts to "fix" your parents can easily be
loaded with your own baggage. Moreover, your insights as a
thinking young adult need tempering. Don't totally unleash
yourself; otherwise you'll quickly cross the line into becoming
your parents' judge, jury, and executioner. That kind of attitude is, well, counterproductive. If you absolutely must say
something, go in humbly, prayerfully. Try not to make them

choke; say it in a way they can swallow. Have *their* best interests at heart, not your own comfort zone.

Thank them for whatever they've done right (1 Thessalonians 5:18).

My parents were strict disciplinarians, so my rebellious hide took a lot of tannings. They were usually fair and never abusive. While in Bible college I went through a period when God himself lovingly corrected me. Trying to sort life out, I did a study on the subject of God's discipline in Hebrews 12:5-11. What I learned there made me thankful for every form of discipline I'd ever received, from both God and my parents. The next time I saw my folks, I told them, "Thanks for working with me and not giving up. I deserved and needed every whupping you ever gave me." Made their day.

Live in a way that makes them shine (Proverbs 10:1).

Every foolish act you've ever been guilty of reflects poorly on your parents—even if they still don't know about it. You've made them look bad. Conversely, every godly achievement in your life makes your parents look great—even if they can't fully appreciate the fact. So save your parents the heartache of having birthed a baby-gone-jerk into this world. Do what's right. Honor God. Make Mom and Dad proud.

For Those in Tough Situations

Some parents, unfortunately, can only be described as abusive. If this has been your experience, the charge to honor your parents presents a difficult challenge. There are no simple answers.

In some cases, the abuse is obvious—at least to those who've suffered it. In other situations, a parent's failure can be more subtle—but still undeniably painful. Whether it's the beatings of a drunken father who loves Jack Daniel's more than his family, or the heart stab of a mother who never said, "I love you," the cuts are real, and the scars run deep.

A parent's unrelenting criticism can cause real damage—much worse than the occasional undeserved "You're grounded for the weekend." A father who walks away from his family is far harder to respect than a dad with an occasional temper problem—but who at least sticks around.

If you've grown up in an atmosphere of abuse, divorce, abandonment, or disillusionment, you've got some long-term healing ahead of you. Honoring parents in your situation may be best focused on one thought: Allow God to teach you to forgive and forbear.

Forgiving deals with past hurts.

Forgiveness boldly says, "My mom [dad] was totally wrong in doing [saying] _____ to me. But because God forgives me, I forgive her [him]." Recognizing that your parents were wrong in certain things is *not* dishonoring them. It's facing the truth head on, "and the truth will set you free" (John 8:32).

As valid as your observations concerning your parents' failures may be, you may never hear the words "I'm sorry" from their lips. Christ can give you the grace to forgive your parents anyway. Let this thought sink deep: *Forgiveness benefits you even more than those you forgive.* It uproots a poisonous weed you don't want growing in your heart: bitterness (Hebrews 12:15). Don't hold out on forgiveness, trying to punish your parents. You'll end up torturing yourself more.

Forbearing deals with ongoing faults.

Forbearance boldly says, "My dad [mom] may never acknowledge the areas I long to see change in. I will love him [her] anyway, forgiving as often as necessary." You may never hear either of your parents say, "I've been wrong in always doing [saying] this to you." Jesus can enable you to graciously bear your parents' faults anyway (Colossians 3:13). And that forbearance will free you to honor your parents in other ways.

The mountain is huge, I know. It can be climbed. I know that, too.

A Final Consideration

Thinking about those words, "that you may enjoy long life on the earth," it makes sense that God would give longevity to people who've learned to honor their parents. Such people are nice. They're not mean, disrespectful, vengeful, or hateful—or any of the things that come with a rebellious heart. This sorry world could sure use some more nice people; they're in short supply. God knows that.

Yep. Better keep that one around on earth for a while.

15

Burnt Out on Phony Christians

(How to handle hypocrisy, inside and out)

Jim walked into Cal's dorm apartment without knocking, just like he'd done many times before. Friends since junior high, the two guys were tight. Jim searched the room's lounge, finding a mess of books, paper, soda cans, and an empty pizza box. A blanket was strewn across an open futon. *Must have had a friend over,* Jim guessed. The absence of a pillow on the lumpy futon struck him as strange.

Raiding the mini-fridge for a soda, Jim could hear the shower running. Snapping a Dr. Pepper, he turned to Cal's bedroom. Its door was firmly closed.

Fast asleep, Jim decided. *We'll take care of that.*

Setting the Dr. Pepper on the floor, Jim quietly turned the knob and opened the door. Just then the shower stopped running. Jim needed to hurry, or this little surprise would be interrupted. Creeping toward the figure buried under the sheets, Jim formed his hands into claws, ready to gouge Cal into consciousness.

But there were a couple of things wrong.

An extra pillow lay discarded on the floor. And the hips under those sheets seemed a little too curved.

The bathroom door opened. Jim snapped his head toward the noise, fingers frozen in space. There stood Cal, in the bedroom doorway, a green bath towel wrapped around his waist.

"C-Cal?" Jim gasped.

"What are you doing here?"

"I'm looking for you."

"Don't you ever knock?" Cal demanded.

Jim stared at his friend, gaping.

The rustling of sheets brought him back to the figure in the bed.

"Cal?" a tiny voice asked. A tangle of blonde hair popped from under the sheets. Long lashes fought to unglue themselves from smudged mascara.

"Ci-Cindy?" Jim asked, barely able to find his voice.

Suddenly Jim felt himself jerked by the arm and dragged from the room. Cal slammed the door shut, kicking over the Dr. Pepper. Snatching the can, he flung it into the steamy bathroom. Aluminum clattered against porcelain, and soda sprayed through the fog.

"Don't you ever come into this apartment again without knocking." Cal's eyes beamed a hatred Jim had never seen before.

His own heart surged with anger. Biting it back, Jim kept his voice low. "What were you doing spending the night alone with Cindy in your apartment?"

"She needed a place to sleep, guy. I slept on the couch. Back off. Now."

Jim paused, heart pounding with doubt. Then he shook his head and dove in. "I don't care if you spent the night across the kitchen table playing Old Maid, this looks bad, Cal. Besides, what's with the extra pillow in your room?"

Cal's face twitched.

"Don't you care what Jesus thinks?" Jim asked, pleading.

The face went cold. "Outta my place, pal." A big thumb pointed the way.

Eyes wide, head down, ears burning, Jim obeyed.

Hamstrung by Hypocrisy

Burnt out by all the hypocrisy you're seeing in the lives of people you thought knew better? You probably have good reason. There's a lot of phony stuff out there, dressed up in people who call themselves Christians.

Some of those people may be your friends.

When you see sin in the hearts of others—and you will—beware. You are in a vulnerable situation. Discouragement will knock on your door. Don't open it. Behind that door, the devil rubs his hands together in evil excitement, rehearsing his sales pitch: "This whole God thing's a farce. It doesn't work. Christianity is full of hypocrites. Give it up."

Don't succumb to discouragement and cynicism. Recognize Satan's lies. Use this painful time to consider some important truths.

Understand this: Not all who call themselves Christians truly are.

Jesus said, "Many will say to me on that day, 'Lord, Lord, did we not prophesy in your name, and in your name drive out demons and perform many miracles?' Then I will tell them plainly, 'I never knew you'" (Matthew 7:22-23).

People who don't truly know Jesus as Savior haven't got the capacity to live like him. Pretend believers, by definition, will be two-faced. Their religion is just an empty shell.

Rest assured: Jesus is no hypocrite.

With your eyes on people—even good people—you'll eventually be disappointed. Guaranteed. And if you gaze 24/7 at the phoniness of others, you're asking for complete disillusionment. You'll see hypocrisy, real or imagined, absolutely everywhere. That's a black place to be.

Instead look at Jesus (Hebrews 12:2-3). You won't find an ounce of hypocrisy, not a flicker of phoniness. He's always pure, consistent, and appropriate, in both history and his present-day dealings in your life. Jesus Christ, the man who knew no sin (2 Corinthians 5:21), is genuine Christianity personified.

Be reminded: You're not alone.

Jesus is painfully aware of hypocrisy, too. He sees its every manifestation far more clearly than your finite eyes can. While on Earth, he dealt with a plague of religious phonies. He called them "whitewashed tombs, which look beautiful on the outside but on the inside are full of dead men's bones" (Matthew 23:27). The history of mankind is crammed with people who claimed to have one set of standards while living out another. There's comfort in knowing you're not alone in your disturbing discoveries. And there's wisdom to be gained from realizing that even though Jesus sees it all—in all its ugliness—he's still patient (Psalm 103:8).

Be sobered: Hypocrisy also lurks within your own soul.

Your own hypocrisy might not be flagrant, but you no doubt have traces of it in your life. Hypocrisy is a subtle sin. Consider these easily-overlooked-but-still-very-ugly faces of phony Christianity:

- Miffed that your roommate never has learned to listen, you cut him off midsentence and let him know.
- Shocked that you witnessed your friend shoplifting,

you prepare a Bible study on the subject with pirated software.

- Flustered at the cheapskate Christians who leave you lousy tips, you go about your Christmas shopping with the nagging fear of running into a Salvation Army man with one of those stupid bells.

- Scandalized by the missionary kid who wears sweaters with necklines way too low, you squeeze into your jeans determined to slip her a little advice on modesty.

- Upset that all the Christians in your dorm are mammoth sloths who think nothing of lying fast asleep on a Sunday morning, you go to church unaware of how much you envy them.

Realize that hypocrisy sprouts in your heart long before it blossoms into hypocritical actions. God's Word says that your heart is "deceitful above all things" (Jeremiah 17:9). That means your heart can outdo the devil himself in making you think you're doing God's will when you really aren't. Only God can unravel the tangled motivations of your soul. You desperately need him to reveal to you your own hypocritical tendencies.

Don't Just Stand There

Don't witness hypocrisy at work without taking action. Take some positive steps.

First Step

Allow God to reveal to you any phoniness in your own life (Psalm 139:23-24). You can't help a guy with his temper if your own heart is fuming. Confess your hypocrisy to God, get a new attitude, make any necessary apologies, and move on, your gaze firmly fixed on Jesus.

Next Step

With your conscience clean—no planks in your own eye (Matthew 7:5)—decide whether God would have you help your friend where his life doesn't measure up.

If you sense a green light, ask God for wisdom on issues like approach and timing. Prayerfully think it through.

Then, before you do anything else, get a necessary dose of humility from this verse: "Brothers, if someone is caught in a sin, you who are spiritual should restore him gently. But watch yourself or you also may be tempted" (Galatians 6:1). "Gently" is key. Don't go into this with a head full of steam. If you do, you'll just burn your friend, leaving wounds that may never heal (Proverbs 18:19).

Third Step

Choose a private moment; you don't want to embarrass anyone in front of others. Then say what needs to be said.

Find courage in this passage: "My brothers, if one of you should wander from the truth and someone should bring him back, remember this: Whoever turns a sinner from the error of his way will save him from death and cover over a multitude of sins" (James 5:19-20).

Fourth Step

Realize that your well-intentioned efforts may draw an angry reaction. You may need to take it further. Matthew 18:15-17 gives some clear direction for difficult situations like this.

Final Step

Whether or not you feel led to confront the problem, avoid sticking your nose in the air the next time you see that person. Instead pray. Learn from his or her folly. Realize that if it wasn't for God's grace, you might be in a worse state. And make your relationship with Jesus so real and attractive that your erring friend will want to come back and join you.

16

Master of Murder, Lord of Lies

(Pointing a finger in the face of Satan's schemes)

"What's the matter, Cunningham?" the voice rumbled over the hallway's din. "Didn't you enjoy my class?"

Steve Cunningham spun on his heel, book bag whirling behind him. "Sorry, sir?"

"My class," his professor repeated, irritated. "Did you not enjoy it?"

"Not particularly, sir. Why?"

"Do you ever enjoy one of my classes?"

"No, sir. I'm afraid not."

The professor drew closer, his eyes a hard squint. "Why did you even select the course if everything I say offends your sensibilities?"

"It's a requirement for my degree." Steve said with a crooked smile, shrugging his shoulders.

"And am I right in thinking that your sensibilities are offended by what I teach?"

"I'm not sure I'd call it 'offended.' I just don't believe most of what you say."

"For example?"

Steve stared at the mixed array of pens and combs in his professor's pocket while his mind raced, searching for an appropriate response. *Lord, help me.*

The professor took another step forward. "For example?"

"Well," Steve began, still grasping. "That bit from Nietzsche, claiming man reaches his highest potential through mastery

of his fellow man—I don't buy it. Pure bunkum in my books."
Steve bit his lip, wishing he'd left out that last bit. "Bunkum"
was this prof's favorite word.

"I see." The words were stiff. "Since you have so summarily
dismissed the philosophies of one of the world's greatest
minds, what is it you *do* accept?" The professor pulled a pen
from his pocket, absently toying with it.

"I go with the words of the greatest mind that ever lived,"
Steve began, scrambling through his memory banks. *What was
that verse, Lord?* He gazed at his toes, desperate for inspiration.

An awkward silence followed. The words wouldn't come.

"Look at me, young man," the professor demanded.

As Steve reluctantly raised his head, the professor tapped
him on the chest with his pen. "Who is this 'greatest mind that
ever lived'?"

Steve swallowed hard. "He's the man who said"—the words
came to him in a flash—"'If anyone wants to be first, he must
be the very last, and the servant of all.' I'll take him over
Nietzsche any day."

"I should have guessed you were a Jesus freak!" the professor spat. Then he paused, gauging Steve's reaction.

Steve wasn't sure what to say. He blinked.

"So, since you follow this purported incarnation of truth,
and since I reject him entirely, you must see me as the king of
liars." The statement was half question, half challenge.

Steve Cunningham shifted the book bag on his shoulder,
ready for a quick escape. "No, sir. Not at all. You're just one of
his unwitting mouthpieces."

A Two-Rabbit Bag

The devil has only two tricks in his repertoire: murder and lies. Jesus described him by saying, "He was a *murderer from the beginning* and has always hated the truth. There is no truth in him. When he lies, it is consistent with his character, for he is a liar and *the father of lies*" (John 8:44, NLT).

However Satan's approach appears on the surface, at its heart it always turns out to be one of these two vicious tactics. Either he's out to kill you, or he's going to try to deceive you. That is helpful to understand.

Master of Murder

Sobered by the thought that Satan wants to kill you? Good. You're obeying God's Word: "Be sober, be vigilant; because your adversary the devil, as a roaring lion, walketh about, seeking whom he may devour" (1 Peter 5:8, KJV).

Drugs, alcohol, and illicit sex are three of his weapons of choice against your age group. If he can't get you to OD, or wrap your pickup around an oak tree, he'll take you slowly with an STD. Those aren't his only weapons, of course. Others include foolish dares, red Corvettes, unnecessary heroics, and bottles of sleeping pills. He's a master assassin.

And he's likely to invite you to your own funeral with some pretty obvious lies:

- "It's risky, yeah. But if you're going to join this fraternity, suck it up and take the challenge."
- "Can't you get this thing to go any faster?"
- "But everyone does this on their twenty-first birthday."

Even Jesus had to ward off Satan's attempt at assassination prior to the cross: "Go ahead and jump. God will send angels to catch you" (Matthew 4:6).

Be sober. Stay sober. Don't get paranoid, but do remember, an angel of death roams nearby.

Lord of Lies

Satan's deceptions are the real challenge. Most Christian youth are mature enough to avoid the pitfalls the devil has laid out to kill them. But when it comes to big fibs and little ones, the snares of Satan are legion.

The instruments the devil uses to propagate his lies are almost as numerous as the lies themselves: music, magazines, movies, TV, radio, theater, newspapers, advertisements, video games, novels, textbooks, professors, talk show hosts, sports celebrities, movie stars, acquaintances, false prophets, well-meaning-but-misled preachers, and false religions and cults—for starters. Oh, don't forget this: www.one-deep-pile-of-bunkum.com.

Understand that the individuals the devil uses usually aren't monsters out to serve you a fat, black lie. That would be too obvious. Instead, Satan sells his deceptions packaged in the guise of nice people, mixed with as much truth as possible. More powerful still, the lies people distribute on the devil's behalf are generally convictions they sincerely accept. That's what makes Satan's scams so believable. The more truth and sincerity your Enemy can mix with any given deception, the more effective it becomes.

Even a good friend can be used to lead you astray. She may have the best of intentions, but the suggestion "That guy is perfect for you" may not come from God. If she goes on to insist that "anything goes, as long as your love for each other is sincere," you can be certain your friend has swallowed a fat hook, one the devil gleefully dangles in your face. The apostle Peter was used by Satan in an attempt to deceive Jesus, the very person Peter longed to serve and follow (Matthew 16:21-23).

It's no great exaggeration to say that the devil tries to "hook" you a thousand times a day.

Unhooking Lies Already Swallowed

Be convinced of this: In your eighteen-plus years of existence, you have swallowed a string of lies. That's not a guilt trip; that's reality. Many of the decisions you make are being jerked around by unseen hooks in your mind. It's impossible, as mere humans, to have completely avoided every one of Satan's shams.

Fully aware of the problem, God wants to take you somewhere: "Let this mind be in you, which was also in Christ Jesus" (Philippians 2:5, KJV). In other words, God wants you to think the way Christ thinks. No lies or deceptions in Jesus' mind. That's a wonderful place to be.

To get you there, God has to do some major renovations. Paul put it this way: "Do not conform any longer to the pattern of this world, but be transformed by the renewing of your mind" (Romans 12:2). God's primary means of bringing about this mind renewal—unhooking the lies, so to speak—is his Word. Only truth can undo untruth. Jesus, while praying for you, asked his Father this: "Sanctify them by the truth; your word is truth" (John 17:17). Here's a loose translation for the phrase "sanctify them": *Get them untangled from Satan's net of deception.*

The degree to which you allow your mind to remain riddled with ideas, values, and slogans that come from the devil is the measure to which your existence will be confusing, empty, and outright miserable. A life based on lies is unhappy. No way around it.

That's why you desperately need—on a steady basis—to meditate on the Scriptures. "Truth will set you free" (John 8:32). The deeper your appreciation of God's Word, the greater your freedom. Don't be passive in your pursuit of truth.

Be hungry.

Satan's Hooks—Out Where You Can See Them

Paul talks about being aware of the devil's schemes (2 Corinthians 2:11). It's sometimes helpful to put your enemy's lies down in black and white, unmasking them for the folly that they are. Here's a short encyclopedia of common falsehoods found today. These are deceptions Satan sells day in, day out. He knows that if he pushes a lie often enough, most people will buy it. If you think you've heard and heeded any of the following sales pitches, allow God's Word to do its job. Root the lie out. Find a true way of thinking.

There is no absolute truth. Anyone who believes otherwise has spent the last fifty years in a cave. Forget about the guy who said, "I am the way and *the truth* and the life. No one comes to the Father except through me" (John 14:6). And never mind the fact that "there is no absolute truth" is a statement that contradicts itself. That's a glitch we'll sort out in our next marketing meeting.

It's all good. Anything works as long as you're sincere about it. Don't think about how ridiculous that sounds; just get out there and go for it. Your heart's in it, so it'll turn out just fine.

"There is a way that seems right to a man, but in the end it leads to death" (Proverbs 14:12). Don't pay attention to that. Death is good, too. Any Goth knows that.

Fitting in is the only thing that matters. So if you're a Christian, keep it low key. Wouldn't want anyone to be asking you about Jesus, would you? Others might overhear, and that would be totally embarrassing.

"I am not ashamed of the gospel, because it is the power of God for the salvation of everyone who believes" (Romans 1:16). Come on! Do you know how many people are listening to you? Any idea the amount of gossip you're generating?

College is for experiencing. So go ahead and dive in. You're free to sample the whole, juicy smorgasbord. Mom's not looking, Dad's not around, and your pastor's too far away to care.

"I want you to be wise about what is good, and innocent about what is evil" (Romans 16:19). Give me a break. How can you know if it's truly evil, if you haven't tried it first? Put that Bible down!

Only once never hurts. No one's ever been killed the first time they enjoyed a meth mirage—at least not according to *my* records. You've never watched a nice horror flick? Get a life! You've gotta see one just to say you *have.*

There's nothing wrong with trying anything once.

"Have you eaten from the tree that I commanded you not to eat from?" (Genesis 3:11). Er, ah, yeah, right. But that was a long time ago.

Halfway does no harm. So if you smoke but don't inhale, how's that a problem? It takes four drinks to get drunk; you can surely handle three—and one little extra sip. Just plagiarize a couple of pages; no one will notice. And if you both keep your clothes on, you can have most of the fun without the guilt, right?

"But let the Lord Jesus Christ take control of you, and don't think of ways to indulge your evil desires" (Romans 13:14, NLT). Who said anything about indulging? Halfway is *not* indulging—really.

Your body is your own. Yours to do with as you please. Have at it. You can always have a doctor fix anything you don't like later.

"You are not your own; you were bought at a price. Therefore honor God with your body" (1 Corinthians 6:19-20). Oh, my, you aren't considering *that* ludicrous option, are you?

Now is all that counts. Does tomorrow *ever* matter? Of course not. Don't give it a second thought. Live for today. Gorge, belch, and be oh-so-merry. Life is short, and then you disappear. Who cares about anything that comes after that?

"Man is destined to die once, and after that to face judgment" (Hebrews 9:27). Would you quit thinking such depressing thoughts!

Knowing is the same as doing. So suck up the sermon. Cram your brain full of Bible trivia. Just don't let them change the way you live—or anything radical like that.

"Do not merely listen to the word, and so deceive yourselves. Do what it says" (James 1:22). Watch out. That Book wants to control your life!

Lazy is cool. So relax until the cows calve horses. You wouldn't want to get too excited about life. Enthusiasm about anything short of meeting Tom Cruise or Gwyneth Paltrow is a waste of energy. Do your absolute best to get maximum results out of minimum action. People will stand amazed at your smooth effortlessness.

"Never be lazy in your work, but serve the Lord enthusiastically" (Romans 12:11, NLT). I'm telling you, that overblown Book will contradict *anything* I have to say.

I don't need to hear that again. Once is plenty, especially when it comes to religious stuff. How many times have you heard: *"For God so loved the world..."*? Blah, blah, blah. Yada, yada, yada. You'd think they were trying to sell you something.

"So I will always remind you of these things, even though you know them and are firmly established in the truth you now have. I think it is right to refresh your memory" (2 Peter 1:12-13). You really know how to make a demon's life miserable, you know that?

Warding Off the Devil's Darts

No matter how many lies Satan has hooked you with already, he does not slow down. The rush of untruth presses on. The devil hasn't merely pawned you lies in the distant past; he continues to attack you with them in the ongoing present.

Consider this verse: "Take up the shield of faith, with which you can extinguish all the flaming arrows of the evil one" (Ephesians 6:16). Those "flaming arrows" are thoughts, little lies, which Satan launches into your mind during the course of a day. He and his fallen host—we're talking millions of demons here—have nothing better to do than run around telling lies, as many and as fast as they can. That's their 24/7 vocation because they don't need to eat, sleep, or take potty breaks. They *like* their job. If your imagination conjures up an imp sitting on your shoulder, whispering sweet, evil little nothings into your ear all day long, that's fine. It's not really like that, but the picture may help you understand. One way or another, Satan and his unholy pals are itching to stick you with their barbs.

Unless you have an active faith—a shield you're constantly holding in ready position—those lies are going to get you. *Whoosh, thunk! Whoosh, thunk! Heh-heh-heh! Stick him some more! Thunk. Thunk. Thunk.*

Now, what does "an active faith" look like?

The Gatekeeper
Second Corinthians 10:5 provides a good model: "We demolish arguments and every pretension that sets itself up against the knowledge of God, and we take captive every thought to make it obedient to Christ."

Think of an active faith as a strict gatekeeper for your mind, one who is deeply concerned about what comes in to occupy it. He wants your brain to be a safe, healthy environment.

Now imagine the thousands of thoughts you have in a day, all lined up, waiting to enter the castle that is your mind. Some of those thoughts bring good tidings and no danger. Others, however, conceal a poisoned dagger.

As each thought steps up, the gatekeeper pulls it aside and frisks it, checking it against truth. *Does this thought help my master in his desire to know God? Will it enable him to obey Christ more?* Your gatekeeper firmly challenges everything you see and hear. *Run that by me again. Is that true? What does God say? I'll have to check it out.*

If a thought or idea passes inspection, it is allowed full entry. But if it is unmasked as a lie, it is taken captive, imprisoned, and not allowed to wander freely in your mind.

Equipping Your Gatekeeper

An active faith—an excellent gatekeeper—is what the Bereans had. After eagerly hearing Paul preach, they "examined the Scriptures every day to see if what Paul said was true" (Acts 17:11). What a great attitude!

You can bet Satan had a hard time fooling them. Their example is yours to follow.

17

Spotting Satan's Smiles

(Knowing a cult when you see one)

He can't believe his eyes.

Not only is she cute but she also has a Bible. It sits on top of her books, right where every God-abhorring student and professor can see. *What guts!* This he has to check out.

He pops three Tic-Tacs, adjusts his collar, and makes his move.

"Hi, my name's Brian." He eases into the library chair opposite her. "Nice Bible. Don't see many of those in this den of iniquity." Brian winces, not sure his attempt at humor will work. A little too preachy, not enough laugh.

She smiles. *What a smile!*

Brian leans forward. "You actually read it?"

"Every day," she says, the smile still perfect.

"Wow, that's impressive!" Great, another Christian at last. "Wish I knew more people like you," he continues, pouring on the charm. He sits back, totally relaxed.

"What's your favorite book of the Bible?" she asks.

Brian feels his face twitch. "Uh, well, er ... Proverbs, I guess." Ouch. Got to read that Book more, starting tomorrow. "Yeah, Proverbs. Good food for the mind, that one." Lame, but, hey, she's still smiling.

"A really helpful book," she agrees.

Brian watches her lips pucker at the word "book," his eyes dreamy. *What a voice. Keep talking, girl.*

"It's helped me make some big decisions."

Brian nods encouragingly, fighting the crazy urge to drop on one knee and kiss her hand. *Nice hands, by the way.*

"But there's another book from God I enjoy even more." She gently pats the Bible, then waits for a response. Cool. She's eager to keep the conversation going.

"Well, I definitely want to hear all about it." *Yeah, like for the next hundred years,* Brian decides. "But before I do, what's your name?"

She smiles afresh. "Marcie." She holds out her hand. "Pleased to meet you, Brian."

The crazy urge strikes again. Brian contents himself with a simple handshake.

That smile is plenty enough.

A Couple of Mistakes

In his puppy dog excitement, Brian made two bad assumptions.

Naive Notion #1

Brian assumed the attraction was mutual, that Marcie liked him as much, he already liked her. He had no idea about the true motives behind that lovely smile.

Dangerous ground, to say the least.

It wouldn't pay to get too paranoid about this, but some religious cults do use physical attraction to draw others into their ranks. The tactic is brazen, but it's done without shame. What seems to start as just a guy-girl thing slowly leads into a web of strange beliefs. Such webs are all the more sticky because of the emotional ties involved. Often the relationship breaks off as the "spider" leaves the new convert heartbroken in order to draw another victim into the web.

You need to carry a healthy skepticism into life, especially when meeting new people. Understand that the world is peppered with manipulators, cheats, and outright seducers. They'll use smiles, flattery, gifts, and even money to win you over, mesmerizing you into their system of belief. Remember, if the devil's in the picture, nothing is what it seems to be.

Brian's supposedly favorite book of the Bible touches on this. "A simple man believes anything, but a prudent man gives thought to his steps" (Proverbs 14:15). "A prudent man sees danger and takes refuge, but the simple keep going and suffer for it" (Proverbs 22:3).

Get prudent. You don't want to suffer in the arms of someone who believes Jesus is Satan's younger brother. Yes, there are people in this world who believe that. Some are good-looking. They smile.

And they even carry a Bible.

Naive Notion #2

That brings us to Brian's even more foolish assumption. He thought that because Marcie read her Bible every day, she must be a Christian. Sorry. That's like saying, "Marcie takes a bath every day. She must be an Olympic swimmer."

Just because a guy carries the *NIV Student Study Bible* doesn't mean he understands it. Remember Nicodemus? He was an influential religious leader in his day, a Bible-toting Pharisee. But while discussing religion, Jesus had to ask him, "You are Israel's teacher, and do you not understand these things?" (John 3:10). Imagine the amazement in Jesus' voice. Jerusalem University's Old Testament professor didn't understand his own textbook.

A wise man once said, "All that glitters is not gold." You may be hungry for a spiritual friend, desperate to spend time with anyone willing to say "God" as anything other than a curse. Great. That's a valid, God-given desire. You need healthy relationships with spiritual people.

But make sure they're *healthy*. Be certain you're dealing with true believers in Jesus—the Jesus of the Bible. Any other "Jesus" is trouble. If you pour out your soul to someone who believes Christ was only an archangel, or merely a moral teacher, you'll get spiritually sick—fast.

The apostle John encourages you to "test the spirits to see whether they are from God, because many false prophets have gone out into the world" (1 John 4:1). In the miasma of religious beliefs circulating today, there is one simple test to distinguish true spiritual gold from the gold of fools.

The Acid Test: Jesus

Jesus is God's Son, equal with God, one with the Father (John 17:20-23). He's the only Way to heaven, the only Truth personified, the only source of eternal life (John 14:6). Only Jesus stands as mediator between God and man (1 Timothy 2:5). He is the King of kings. At his awesome Name every knee will bow (Philippians 2:10). When it comes to true faith, Christ is the beginning, the end, and everything in between (Hebrews 12:2).

This is the Jesus of the Bible. No name demands greater reverence or worship. The Bible lifts Jesus high, extolling him as supreme.

And Satan hates it. Invariably, every cult the devil has ever spawned attacks Christ's exalted position. Satan seeks to drag

Jesus down any way he can. He wants you to think Jesus was a mere man who gradually made himself a god. If that doesn't work, the devil will get you to focus on "the christ within," the Jesus from Jupiter, or a Savior in army fatigues.

Satan doesn't care which deception you choose, as long as you don't see Jesus as the almighty Second Person of the Trinity, seated at the right hand of the Father, existent in eternity past, all you need for your earthly joy and heavenly acceptance. Paul says it even better: "For in Christ the fullness of God lives in a human body, and you are complete through your union with Christ. He is the Lord over every ruler and authority in the universe" (Colossians 2:9-10, NLT).

The devil's masks are many, but their design has one common element: present the Living Word, Jesus Christ, as less than what the Written Word, the Bible, claims him to be. In understanding that, you have your acid test: *Is Jesus exalted to the highest by what this person believes?*

If the answer isn't a loud *yes*, you're dealing with a perversion of truth. A cult. Something to be rejected.

So get to know Jesus. When you read your Bible, see him on every page. Imagine him high on a cross, high up in heaven, high on the throne. Make it an adventure to discover the splendor of Jesus. The more you discover, the higher your heart will lift him, the more he'll draw you to himself (John 12:32).

And the less likely you'll be seduced by one of Satan's smiles.

18

Money Under My Mattress

(And other ways of staying financially free)

The idea seemed strange to me, but I couldn't wait to try it out. I was in my senior year at Bible school, and most days I was as poor as a church mouse on a long vacation. But right then, with 150 bucks worth of small bills in my hands, I felt mildly rich.

The married students whose trailer I was about to visit weren't home. I knew that. That's why I was going. The only person present was their twelve-year-old son, Alan. He knew what was happening, so he let me inside.

Swearing Alan to secrecy, I searched for good places to hide the money. Nothing too hard—I wanted it all to be found. Slipping each bill into its hiding spot, I smiled. This was so much fun. They'd be finding this stuff for weeks. They sure needed it.

And it didn't seem to matter that I was giving away everything I had.

Two months later my friend John slapped me on the back, his wife smiling beside him. "We found another five bucks today. It just keeps coming and coming, you rascal."

I cracked a grin. I was still poor, but I'd learned a big lesson: Happiness can be mine without a lot of money.

Crashing on Their Cash

In Turkey, where banks aren't a trusted institution, it's rumored that people have a total of sixty billion dollars squirreled away under their mattresses. When it comes to money, people in that country think about the future.

Most students in North America, however, are blithely wandering into a future of debt. The average law graduate leaves university with an $80,000 student loan debt. Nineteen out of twenty students use credit cards, carrying an average balance of $3,000. More than 85 percent of students are concerned about their money situation, most claiming that financial worries adversely affect academic performance. Big debt means bad grades.

That doesn't need to describe you.

God and Money

Understand that money, in itself, is not evil. Jesus freely used it while he walked among us (Matthew 17:25-27). He even recommended using money in order to make friends (Luke 16:9). No, money isn't the problem. It's *loving* money that will twist your soul (1 Timothy 6:10).

The Bible is full of practical advice on dealing with dollars. It's one of God's favorite subjects, because he knows you desperately need help managing your finances. Heed his advice and you'll save yourself major stress. Ignore God's tips at the risk of your sanity.

Money is a Bible study you'll want to pursue now because money is a subject that will chase you throughout life. A handful of biblical pointers have served me well in the twenty years since I graduated from high school. As a missionary I'm still comparatively poor—but I also have zero debt, which makes me richer, in a way, than almost everyone I know.

For what they're worth, I'll pass my ideas along.

I take no shame in working for money.

Work is good, and good work deserves to be paid (1 Timothy 5:18). As a missionary I depend on other people's generosity, but I also do whatever possible to supplement that income.

Paul, a fellow missionary and my #2 hero (Jesus is my #1), serves as a great example of the healthy work ethic I long to imitate:

> We were not idle when we were with you, nor did we eat anyone's food without paying for it. On the contrary, we worked night and day, laboring and toiling so that we would not be a burden to any of you. We did this, not because we do not have the right to such help, but in order to make ourselves a model for you to follow. For even when we were with you, we gave you this rule: "If a man will not work, he shall not eat."
>
> 2 THESSALONIANS 3:7-10

Do you see the positive attitude Paul had toward work as he slaved away with a smile sewing tents after the sun went down? In a lazy world that increasingly hates work, a love for honest labor is an attitude I want to cultivate.

I am in no rush to get rich.

Proverbs 28:20 makes it plain: "A faithful man will be richly blessed, but one eager to get rich will not go unpunished." Life is not about getting rich; money is a means to maintain life, no more. If God provides extra cash, great—I'll have more to serve him with. If I have to get by on less, that's fine— I can still be richly content (1 Timothy 6:6).

My goal shouldn't be to get rich but to fulfill God's perfect plan for my life. With that thought occupying my mind, I'll easily ignore temptations to play the lottery or to sign up for the latest pyramid sales scheme. The vast majority of people who go down get-rich-quick paths, like the above Proverb says, take a beating.

I am allergic to debt.

The very thought of it makes me break out in goose pimples. If I don't have the money to spend, I don't spend it. I appreciate brainless choices like that—there are too many other decisions in life I actually have to think about. Again, Paul has great input on this point: "Let no debt remain outstanding, except the continuing debt to love one another" (Romans 13:8).

For those in the awkward situation of having to secure student loans, I encourage you: Manage those debts well. Make it your goal and prayer to pay them off ASAP. And don't add to your burden by carrying unreasonable credit card debt. If you have a problem that way, use your Visa to buy a sharp pair of scissors, then cut the card into tiny pieces.

I don't buy without my wife's consent.

Even when money's available, I still need help with my buying decisions. Proverbs 12:15 says, "The way of a fool seems right to him, but a wise man listens to advice." Was Solomon thinking about money there?

Not every possible purchase that pops into my brain is a good idea. Seeking out the counsel of my wife and closest earthly friend, I save all kinds of money by not making dumb deals. And Beth comes to me for the same input. Often we simply decide to hold off on a purchase, only to discover a month later that we never really needed it.

I have fallen in love with generosity.

I find that with a giving attitude, I am much less inclined to spend money on myself. Instead I find little ways to save so there's more to share. Then, in giving away, I free myself from always having to *have*. And giving money away is as much fun as ever. Generosity really is a more blessed way to live (Acts 20:35).

Since my calling has me living in a poor part of Mexico, that makes me a rich *gringo* in the minds of my neighbors. And compared to 98 percent of the world, I *am* rich. Paul has specific counsel for rich people like you and me:

Command those who are rich in this present world not to be arrogant nor to put their hope in wealth, which is so uncertain, but to put their hope in God, who richly provides us with everything for our enjoyment. Command them to do good, to be rich in good deeds, and to be generous and willing to share. In this way they will lay up treasure for themselves as a firm foundation for the coming age, so that they may take hold of the life that is truly life.

1 TIMOTHY 6:17-19

Wow! Lots to chew on there. One thing is certain: With all the good deeds and generous sharing my money could accomplish, it probably isn't a good idea to hide it under my mattress.

19

Gambling Is for Losers

(For poor souls dying to make a fast buck)

One minute to go, and the jerk sportscaster was way too excited. So was everyone else in the room. Miami had just scored a touchdown, putting them ahead by five points. Popcorn flew through the air as guys made diving receptions on the sofa. When they shifted to catching with their mouths, the noise escalated, popcorn falling on the carpet like hail.

With mouths as big as theirs, you would think they could make a completion. The morons. Daniel fidgeted with the MasterCard in his hand. Dallas had to beat the Dolphins by three and a half or he'd be out $320. He always bet opposite his friends. More often than not he won. Today he'd boldly covered everyone's wager—Daniel could still see their eyes popping—but now he was going to take it square and hard on the chin. Worse still, he'd used his dad's credit card to drum up a stake.

"Computer World, I'm yours!" a female voice yelled above the noise. "Daniel's going to buy me MechWarrior 5—aren't you, Daniel?" Karla Dillingsworth was cute but totally tomboy. *What was a girl doing gambling, anyway? Any excuse to be around guys? Whatever.*

Daniel scowled while the Cowboys launched a last-minute drive. Too little, too late. He watched Karla pump her fist at the TV, shrieking like a banshee. It was usually nice to have her around but not right now. Besides, Daniel had better places to be.

Like the Domino Palace.

Twelve seconds to go and Dallas scored, winning by two. But they were supposed to win by three and a half. *The losers.* The missing two points would cost him 320 bucks.

The MasterCard in his hand folded in half with a snap. He stared at it as if someone had died.

Suddenly they were all around him, their smelly, popcorny hands sticking in his face. Daniel reached into his pocket, counted the money, and threw it across the room, most of it falling behind the sofa. Everyone but Karla scrambled for his winnings.

"You all right?" Karla asked.

Daniel stood quiet, trying to unkink the credit card.

"You'll win it back. No time. Guaranteed. It all goes and comes around, you know that." Karla punched his shoulder, but Daniel brushed her off and walked out of the house. It would be a while before he exchanged bets with those lame-brains again.

Jumping on his mountain bike, Daniel rode off, determined to shake the loss. He'd crashed and burned before. But he'd also rushed some major digits together.

As the wind raced by his ears, he felt the old, smooth feeling flow over him like warm oil. Oh, yes. This was it. When Daniel felt like this, he hardly ever lost. Lady Luck was tapping him on the shoulder, blowing sweet nothings into his ear. The Cowboys worked the bad luck out of his system. Now for some serious high rolling.

The Domino had plenty of that.

There was just one obstacle: Daniel had eighty bucks in his pocket, but he needed a bigger stake. His bike would do for now. He'd pawn it, then win enough to buy it back in a couple of hours.

Daniel rode into the parking lot of Leon Bickle's Pawn & Cash Exchange, the flashing neon sign of the Domino Palace a minute's walk away.

In the distance stood the spire of Daniel's home church. Seeing it used to bother him, but he had long since ceased to notice.

A Clear Look at the Domino Palace

People who want to get rich fall into temptation and a trap and into many foolish and harmful desires that plunge men into ruin and destruction. For the love of money is a root of all kinds of evil. Some people, eager for money, have wandered from the faith and pierced themselves with many griefs.

1 TIMOTHY 6:9-10

Among other things, God had gambling in mind when he inspired Paul to write those words. Gambling is a mine-field of danger. It stands like a house of horrors for those who dare enter. It tortures its victims with a fever, a sickness that has no earthly cure.

Is gambling a real problem for youth? You bet. Several researchers who surveyed 1,700 students from six colleges and universities found that 33 percent of males and 15 percent of females gambled once a week or more. For many of them the Internet is the game of choice—"www" has come to mean "World Wide Wager."

One person has said, "Gambling is the sure way of getting nothing for something." Here are the reasons why. And as you read, understand that though the names are changed, the stories included are true.

Even when you win, you lose.

Gamblers who win for the first time invariably try again. They're convinced that "luck" will score once more. At first it may, but when Lady Luck disappears, most gamblers feverishly chase their bets, and things go from wrong to really wrong. Rarely does someone win big and walk away, never to return.

Not too long ago nineteen-year-old Gregg Wilson won $30,000 at blackjack over three months. Then he started losing. A few weeks later, having dropped two-thirds of his winnings, he was desperate. In one night he lost the last $10,000 in a red-eyed roulette spree.

It's a quick way to wager away your pals.

Gamblers can shed friends faster than they do money. As losers they generally are miserable, desperate to hit up others for loans to pay gambling debts. Then they find themselves isolated, their buddies suddenly scarce. And welched bets among friends always result in bitterness, sometimes in violence.

You take your chances with addiction.

Nearly one in ten youth develops an addiction toying with the tables—or with lotto, bingo, craps, five-card stud, coin pitching, sports pools, scratch-and-win games, pull tabs, faro, racetracks, or Powerball. The variety could mesmerize anyone. Some students are so hooked that they'll put ten bucks on whether the next person to appear has brown eyes or blue.

Bradley Thompson had a gambling problem that eventually

cost him his chance to go to college. He had to settle for grunt work to pay off a $20,000 gambling debt.

The high-stakes world is full of cheaters and liars.

Bookies make their money by "shifting the lines" in their favor. Occasionally too many people bet the winner. When that happens, bookies often disappear to set up shop elsewhere, leaving the winners as losers. Some simply decide not to pay, smiling in your face instead. They may scare off your business, but there's always another sucker around.

Gamblers tend to exaggerate stories about their winnings and go mute over their losses. No one likes to admit he's a loser. The whole scene is self-deceiving hype—all glitter and no gold.

It may kill you.

Nine out of ten problem gamblers consider suicide. Bradley Thompson sure did. Killing himself seemed like the easiest escape from his $20,000 debt. By working it off instead, he's chosen the smart road. Sad he didn't find the smart road earlier.

One addict in six will attempt suicide. Gregg Wilson succeeded. After losing his last $10,000, he went home, took a shotgun, and ended it all.

Dead broke.

Where Are Your Eyes Fixed?

God doesn't want your heart set on riches. He wants your heart set on his Son, Jesus Christ. The two don't mix. Gambling is inherently a fixation on money. If you want true riches—ones that don't make like a bird and fly away—be fixed on Christ.

Paul, after warning Timothy of the dangers in loving money, continued, "But you, man of God, flee from all this, and pursue righteousness, godliness, faith, love, endurance and gentleness. Fight the good fight of the faith" (1 Timothy 6:11-12).

Christ is coming back. A life lived in obedience to him has a payoff that involves no debt, no guilt, and no gamble—a jackpot that lasts forever.

Guaranteed.

Back to Our Story

Leon Bickle's Pawn & Cash Exchange was long closed when Daniel finally left the Domino. He rubbed the sleep from his eyes, trying to spot a taxi in the neon lights.

What a rush he'd had. Tomorrow he'd come back and get his bike, riding off with a wad of change to spare.

Two guys in dark jackets came toward him. Daniel had seen them watching while he ran up the numbers at the wheel.

He couldn't find a taxi.

He walked faster.

So did the two behind him.

Daniel had heard about the recent mugging near the Domino. He had dismissed it as one of those things that happened only to other people. Of course, he'd never left the Domino a winner before. Strange how clearly the realization came to him now.

Winners were targets.

It was over before Daniel had the chance to yell.

On the ground, the back of his head bleeding, his money gone, he thought about his mountain bike. His stomach lurched with regret. Leon Bickle would probably sell it before Daniel ever got out of the hospital.

Barely conscious now, he saw the blurry outline of a cross on top of a church spire, silhouetted against the light of a full moon.

Daniel closed his eyes, glad of the reminder.

20

No Time to Waste

(Counsel when caught in a red-eyed rush)

Having survived the initial shock of separation from friends and family, I was ecstatic about being at Bible college. I had a bunch of new friends, soccer was one of the school's favorite sports, I was part of student council, and someone picked me for the yearbook staff. Called me a *photojournalist.* Life was grand, a revolving door of grunts on the soccer field and gabfests in the cafeteria lounge—between photo shoots and yearbook writing gigs, of course. No boring moments in my life. My days just flew.

In the midst of all this blinding activity, school assignments were a low priority.

Allow me a short flashback: As an *A* student in high school, I found homework a cinch. Every assignment, regardless of when the teacher handed it out, was completed the night before it was due. Ask my parents. No research, no rewrites. Rip it off, hand it in, take my *A,* thank you very much. It meant a few all-nighters, but, hey, school's kind of cool when experienced through the mental fog of a night with no sleep.

But now my college insisted on lights-out at 11:00 P.M. They enforced the rule with a crew of dorm proctors, students who hopefully had more integrity than I did at the time. No more all-nighters for me, at least in theory.

I had to do a 2,500-word paper for my Genesis teacher, a professor I really respected. The assignment was due—surprise, surprise—the next day. It was 7:00 P.M.—perhaps time to start thinking about tackling this project.

I tore in, but by 11:00 I wasn't even close to finishing. I had to write a decent paper. This professor wasn't going to be as easily scammed as some of my teachers in the past.

An evil thought entered my mind. I ran with it.

Swearing my roommate to secrecy, I took the blankets from my bed. With one I covered our window. With the other I sealed off the crack under our door. Then I turned the light back on, sat down, and kept working. I finished at 5:30 A.M., just in time to take a cold shower and head for breakfast.

"Did you hear what happened to Hamilton?"

Shaking the fog, I perked my ears.

"He was working all night on some Genesis assignment. Proctor caught him at two in the morning. That guy's campused, for sure."

My college was awesome, but it was also strict. "Campused" meant four hours of Saturday morning penal labor on the campus farm, followed by a weekend in the dorm. No social engagements allowed.

Hearing the news about poor Hamilton, I felt bad. God's Spirit knocked on my heart's door. *Insistently.* Before the day was over, I confessed my truancy to both the men's dean and my Genesis professor. They appreciated my honesty but still felt the need to discipline me. I got campused and lost a grade on the paper I'd submitted.

That was my last all-nighter, for sure.

As I slugged away the next Saturday morning, mucking out calf pens, I decided it was time to take a new look at my use of time.

A Skewed Attitude

A quick search on Amazon.com reveals 1,641 books on the subject of time management. It is a perennially hot topic because people are always hungry for tips on "how to save time." Students, juggling the responsibilities of school, work, and an active social life, are some of the most frequent customers. If time hasn't become an issue for you, it soon will be. Wait until you discover the chilling thrill of finals week.

Having read several time-management books myself, I've come to a conclusion: The goal of "saving time" is inherently a selfish one. Think about it. What are we so eager to save time *for?* To go and have more fun, right? Right.

With unbridled fervor, we seek to multitask all the mundane aspects of life—dishes, homework, sleep, that oh-so-boring job—into one tight, efficient bundle, then get it all done in five minutes so we can get back to our driving purpose in life: more fun!

Admit it. We're addicted.

I enjoy computer games. I could vanish for a month in *Rogue Spear,* a tactical rescue game for SWAT fanatics. It seems kind of juvenile for an old man like me to even *want* to do something like that—the game's still wrapped in cellophane on my shelf, beckoning me—but realize this: I've been fed a long line for all my thirty-plus years of life: *Fun is everything.*

Am I knocking fun? Not per se. What I'm concerned about is seeing fun as the number-one push for rushing through all of life's other facets, as if a weekend at Six Flags or Canada's Wonderland were the true source of happiness. It isn't.

Would another of the devil's slogans help make the point here?

Thank God it's Friday.

Now *that* is a rotten attitude about time. As if Monday through Thursday were a complete waste of your existence. Is there no significance to having waited tables for three nights at Denny's, worked hard on two term papers, and washed seven days' worth of laundry? And what about all the other things you get done in a week? Is that all worth *nothing?* The devil would have you think so.

Hand in glove with this T.G.I.F. mentality comes the big hype that hits campus hallways every Monday morning. "What did *you* do over the weekend?" That question is *loaded*. If you didn't see *The Producers* on Broadway, go visit a friend on her personal yacht, or spend a couple of days at a European castle, you're labeled a boring Neanderthal. That is bogus. The pressure to have a social life that outshines that of Julia Roberts is going to run you ragged.

It's time to take a new look at this issue.

Moving Toward a Healthy Attitude

Even though a day has only twenty-four hours, there is enough time for all God wants you to do. "There is *a time for everything, and a season for every activity under heaven*" (Ecclesiastes 3:1). Read this slowly: God—doesn't—want—you—stressed—about—time. Every time you are, let that raise a red flag in your mind: *I need an attitude adjustment, Lord. Where?* He may use one of the following biblical principles to unshackle your thinking:

Give God your to-do list (Proverbs 16:3).

As you stare at that daunting date book, invest a little time asking your Father about each item. He'll gladly make some helpful suggestions: *That one's absolutely unnecessary; scratch it off. You can leave that project for December. Call Janine; she'll help you with that problem. That job you'd better jump on.* No matter how insignificant the task seems to you, God is truly interested in being part of it.

You have permission to say no (James 5:12).

Not every person who has cool ideas about how you should spend your time is sent by God. Don't bow to the pressure of saying yes to every invitation that comes your way. Be gracious about it, but learn to say no. They'll get over it.

Every day could use some gusto (Romans 12:11).

We all need a little more zeal, an extra shot of spiritual fervor, enabling us to move into life's demands at something faster than a slug's pace. Where this hits me is when I get dressed in the morning. It can take me half an hour to mosey my way into a pair of pants and a shirt. I'm a guy! Guys should be able to get dressed in five minutes! And with a squirt of God-given gusto, I do, freeing me to spend my time on more important things.

Your days are numbered (Psalm 90:12).

This simple realization can motivate you to squeeze the most out of every moment, trusting Jesus for wisdom as you go.

A good night's sleep is allowed (Psalm 127:2).
God wants you to enjoy deep rest more than once a month. If you're cutting yourself short to "save time," it'll cost you down the road. Think things through. Make a different sacrifice.

God wants to wean you.
"Everything is permissible—but not everything is beneficial. Everything is permissible—but not everything is constructive" (1 Corinthians 10:23). When it comes to fun, God is a whole lot more permissive than some unhappy (read: mildly constipated) people make him out to be. But with maturity you'll realize that fun *isn't* everything. The day you allow God to wean you from an addiction to fun, you'll have all kinds of time for the more beneficial, constructive aspects of life.

Balance is key (Proverbs 11:1).
Satan is always pushing you toward extremes, particularly in your use of time. Nine hours downloading music files from the Internet? You may want to rethink that. Learn the wholesome happiness of a balanced life, one that gives each of your God-given responsibilities its proper measure of attention. Be honest in how you weigh time.

Everything Jesus did was right on time (Galatians 4:4).
He would love to give you the same experience. Get to know him more; he'll show you how.

21

Living Above the Little Sins

(Recovering the lost art of integrity)

The Mexican drug lord hardly knew what was going on inside of him. I had taught him God's Word weekly in his home for over a year. Jesus Christ was becoming a real person to him, someone he wanted to trust. When you're a marijuana marketer, there are not too many people you *can* trust.

He and his wife had just eaten in a small restaurant. The waitress came back with the change, and they stepped outside, heading for their truck. Counting the money in his hand, the drug lord stopped in his tracks.

"Honey, this change is off. That girl gave us more money than I handed her to start with."

They looked at each other, pondering their good fortune. Then my Mexican friend shook his head. "I've gotta take this back and get it right." He spun on the heel of his ostrich-skin cowboy boot and returned to the restaurant.

The waitress couldn't believe it.

Neither could my Mexican brother and his wife. "Did I just do that?" he asked her, stepping back outside. She smiled, lifted her eyebrows, and nodded. They walked to the truck, very aware that Jesus was doing something in their hearts. With time, Christ would give them the courage to walk away from the whole drug scene.

They had learned a lesson in integrity.

Never Heard of the Word

Integrity has become such an old-fashioned concept that most people don't even know what it means. Webster's defines it as "firm adherence to a code of moral values." I prefer to look at integrity in simpler terms: "honesty in the little things—even after dark."

Though integrity was once a cherished character trait, it has been eclipsed by another value, "success at any cost." Honesty for honesty's sake is no longer cool. Most people are now honest only to the degree that they know someone is looking over their shoulder. If they think they can get away with something, they will. We're talking zero integrity.

The Dividends of Integrity

As believers—if we're wise—we realize that Someone is always looking over our shoulder (Psalm 139:1-12). Integrity should be hugely valuable to us, just as it is to God. We're foolish if it isn't.

Though integrity may cost you—like having to give back a bundle of undeserved change—it might help to understand that integrity also pays. Consider the following benefits of an honest life in the little things:

Integrity protects (Psalm 25:21). There are times when a reputation for meticulous honesty can save your skin. Satan is always trying to get Christians into more trouble than they deserve. A shady lifestyle, even on a few small points, makes it easy for the devil to build a huge, ugly case. But true integrity leaves the devil with no handhold to grab. Check out how Daniel's integrity stood firm when he was faced with the conspiracies of corrupt government officials; the only case they could build against him was based on his relationship with God (Daniel 6:1-5).

Integrity upholds (Psalm 41:12). There's nothing so weak-kneed as a conscience loaded with the guilt of a thousand small compromises. Learn integrity. Then you'll have no unnecessary baggage when tough times hit. God himself will gladly hold you up.

Integrity guides (Proverbs 11:3). A life of little dishonesties makes for complicated thinking. *Should I cover this with another lie, or do I have to come clean before this gets too hairy? Is anyone watching? Do they have any clue about the last time I fudged this?* All that illicit worry is hard on the system—and God wants no part of it. You're on your own.

In contrast, integrity provides a moral compass that makes for lighthearted, no-hassle decisions. *This is the honest thing to do, so the decision is a no-brainer.* Integrity makes life simple. Moreover, you don't need a good memory if you always tell the truth. And Jesus is right there, rooting for you the whole way.

Choosing integrity definitely pays a whole lot more than it costs.

Case Studies in Integrity

The opportunity to exercise integrity shows up in many situations. Give these some thought:

- You bought a term paper over the Internet for "research" purposes, but never quite got around to writing that paper yourself. Now you're out of time. You approach the professor's desk, the plagiarized paper in hand. Will you toss it in the garbage and ask for an extension, even though it costs you a grade?

- You're given a cool CD, only to discover it's been pirated. Do you give it back, saying you can't accept it, risking the awkwardness?

- You're writing an exam when you're handed a cheat sheet to pass down the line. Do you pass it back to the person who handed it to you, ready to face the coming heat?

- You promise to share your testimony at a small Bible study, but something more "interesting" comes up an hour before. Do you turn the new opportunity down and stick with the plan, knowing that keeping your word can sometimes hurt (Psalm 15:1-4)?

- The pop machine malfunctions, giving a free soda to anyone who wants it. Do you settle for water and report the problem to the office?

- You really need that job, but you lack experience. Your friend suggests an "enhancement" on your resumé, insisting everyone does it, and employers expect it. Do you refrain, leaving your need for work in God's hands?

- You're on the yearbook staff, and "it's understood" that the photocopier is available for more than just yearbook work. Do you walk away from the temptation to do "a few personal copies—within reason, of course"?

- You've ordered from Lands' End, and you love the new clothes that came in the mail. But for some strange reason, eight months later the check you sent still isn't cashed. Do you call them up and let them know?

- You see a sign: *Keep off the grass.* Do you walk around?

- You work evenings in a bakery, only to discover that the whole crew knocks off an hour before the shift truly ends. Do you grab a broom and keep your hands busy, willing to face the coming ridicule, ready to tell them why?
- You find a wallet with no ID and a fistful of money. Before claiming the cash, do you make an honest effort to identify the owner?
- You've got eighty miles to go and one hour to get there, but the speed limit is only 55. How fast do you drive?
- You're the treasurer of a campus club—and short on cash. But a $1,000 check is coming to you in the mail. A temporary "loan" to yourself would make life easy. Do you take the hard road?
- You've broken a school rule. Do you confess it to the proper authorities?
- The soccer fullback has just clipped your shin for the third time without drawing a foul. Do you swallow the desire to take a dive?
- You sense that what you're hearing is pure gossip. Do you calmly but courageously say so?
- You crack a small vase in your friend's bathroom. Do you tell her and offer to pay for it?
- The story is good, but it could be even better. Do you say no to exaggeration and tell it like it happened?

One Last Question

She was bereaved and bitter, but Job's wife asked a most important question which applies to us all: "Are you still holding on to your integrity?" (Job 2:9). If we're honest—there's that word again—we'll have to admit to having areas where we still need to *find* integrity before we can hold on to it.

That's where Jesus—the man of perfect integrity (1 John 3:5)—comes in. Enjoy and obey Jesus and integrity will be yours (1 John 3:6). And once it's yours, hold on. Keep enjoying and obeying.

22

The Temptation to Be "Large and in Charge"

(A positive take on submission)

Keith gazed aimlessly into the job fair's mass of buzzing humanity. What a waste of time this was. Self-important management types with designer suits and overstuffed briefcases being fawned over by dressed-to-impress students. And for what? A chance at a $40,000 basement job that demanded another decade of fawning so a guy could earn maybe $60,000. Forget it.

Keith was too smart for that.

The thought made him want to tear the name tag off his shirt: *Keith Lonergan: Engineering (3.9)*. Whose lame idea was it to put every student's grade point average on his or her chest like some tattoo?

A little guy in blue coveralls was looking at Keith's tag. What on earth was *he* doing here? Now the man stared straight at Keith, beady eyes like lasers.

"Keith. I got a son named Keith. He likes to fish."

"Does he?" Keith tried to smile politely.

"Yeah, caught himself an eight-pound largemouth last Friday. Boy, was he happy. What do you like to do?" The little man had a machine-gun mouth with a thick New England accent. It would be interesting just to listen to him.

"Oh, I don't know. Surf the Web. Think big thoughts."

"Oh, yeah? I just got me one of them EZ WebSurfers. Now

I can write these little e-notes to my nephew Dominic in New Jersey, and it don't even cost me nuthin'. He writes me back all the time."

The little man's head bobbed with impish excitement, lost in his own world. Then he twisted his head around like a bird and squinted at Keith. "What kind of big thoughts you been having?"

Keith licked his lips, trying to hide his amusement. "Oh, sometimes I think about starting my own business."

"Start your own business? Whadaya wanna do that for? Any idea the *headaches*?"

"Can't be near the headaches a guy would have working for someone else."

The beady eyes glittered. "What makes you say that?"

"Well, you know. Having to take commands from some old grump with a cheap hairpiece and a cheesy tie who only cares about skinning sixty-eight hours a week out of you so the wannabe company he runs doesn't sink like an Italian battleship. Forget it. Not for me."

The little man's cackling laughter filled the air. Keith smiled nervously, wondering too late if the man came from Sicily or Venice. The features were right.

"Hey, they ain't all of them that bad, son. Take it from me." Grabbing a pen and small pad from his coverall pocket, the little man slashed a quick line across the page. Then he walked away.

Keith stared after him, head shaking. Suddenly a nametag cut off his view: *Benton Hurley: Engineering (3.7)*.

"Were you just talking to that guy?"

"Yeah," Keith replied. "Weird little twerp."

"Did he have a son named Keith who likes to fish?"

Keith stared in amazement. "Yes."

"Well, he's got a son named Benton, too, who just caught himself an eight-pound bass last Friday."

Keith licked his lips, afraid to breathe. "What are you saying?"

"That 'little twerp' is the CEO of Dominic Enterprises. Anyone who gets a job with him starts at $85,000! And he wants to see me again! I still can't believe it." Benton wandered off in a daze.

Gazing over the crowd, heart racing, Keith caught one last glance of the little man in blue coveralls. He was standing by the open door of a long, gray limousine. For an instant the beady eyes beamed Keith's way.

The little man waved good-bye and stepped inside. The door closed behind him.

Wanting What's Not Ours to Have

Ever hear the story about the twenty-two-year-old guy who started up an Internet business and then sold it for $200,000,000? Yeah, well, so has everyone else. And if we were honest, we'd have to confess a mild-to-major twitch of envy. Ever dream of being Bill Gates? Neither have I. But it sure would be nice if he'd put my name on his list of needy charities.

There's something inside of us that craves to be so rich that we'd never have to do what anyone else says again. Ever. Deep down, we long to be large and in charge.

That's a scary attitude to have. Why? Well, if you boil it down to its basic elements, you end up with something 100 percent demonic: *I want to be God.*

Think about it. God is the only being who is truly "large and in charge." He's the only one in the entire universe who, if he wanted to, could completely ignore what everyone else says. No one can boss him around. God does what he wants. It's his right.

And no one else has that right. Only God is God.

But all kinds of beings claim his throne, nevertheless. Lucifer did, thinking himself equal to God (Isaiah 14:14). In allowing his heart to become so twisted, he became the devil. Then he tempted Eve with the same thing: "You will be like God" (Genesis 3:5). Eve took the bait. She wanted to be God. So did Adam. Silly people.

We've all wanted to be God ever since (Romans 5:12).

So you don't like the idea of having to work for *anyone?* You need to wonder where that's coming from.

Understanding Submission

There is one attitude that is absolute death to the ugly thing inside you that screams to be God. Understand and accept *submission,* and that little voice is gone. Reject submission, and you play the devil's game.

Jesus once met a soldier who understood submission, way down deep. While asking Jesus to heal one of his servants, this Roman centurion said, "Lord, I do not deserve to have you come under my roof. But just say the word, and my servant will be healed. For I myself am a man under authority, with soldiers under me." Jesus was so astonished at this man's words, he said, "I tell you the truth, I have not found anyone in Israel with such great faith" (Matthew 8:5-13).

The Submissive Soul

Read the whole story of Jesus and the centurion, and then chew on the following ideas. They should help you understand submission.

Submission knows that Jesus is in charge. Check out the first word from the centurion's mouth: *Lord.* The centurion saw in Jesus the right to rule, even over his servant's sickness. He accepted that. A submissive soul is to recognize who is in command in any given situation. Moreover, such a soul continuously sees Christ as supreme and acts accordingly.

Submission is humble. The centurion did not demand Jesus' help. He humbly yet boldly stepped up and asked for it: "I do not deserve, ... but just say the word." Submission does not mean being too fearful to suggest a good idea to your boss. If you can think of something that will get the job done better, ask for it with quiet confidence. But a lack of submission will have you throwing your weight around, demanding your way. That'll make you zero friends and all kinds of enemies.

Submission recognizes a chain of command. No matter how high up the ladder you climb, there's always someone with greater authority. The centurion had no trouble accepting the fact that he wasn't the ultimate big cheese: "I myself am a man under authority." Great attitude. There are people out there who have the God-given right to tell you what to do. The sooner you accept that, the fewer bumps you'll suffer along the way.

Here are some examples of God-ordained chains of command:

- Christ as head of the Church (Ephesians 1:22-23)
- elders over congregation (Hebrews 13:17)
- husband over wife (Ephesians 5:22-23)
- parents over children (Ephesians 6:1-4)
- government over citizens (Romans 13:1-7)
- employer over employee (Ephesians 6:5)

Submission serves those under authority. The centurion didn't fly around on some power trip. He had compassion for those under his care. He was *concerned* about his servant. When submission is truly understood by all, there is no fear of anyone being *over* anyone because true leadership tenderly serves those being led (John 13:13-15).

Submission is a faith thing. The Roman soldier placed himself under Christ's authority, willing to do whatever Jesus directed in order to see his servant healed. Somewhere in that act of submission was the element of faith that so impressed Jesus.

Many people do what they're told because they're afraid of the big stick. That's not submission, that's subservience. It's outward obedience mixed with inward rebellion. True submission is not forced but *willing*, something done because you believe in the principle of submission. It's motivated by a love for God, not the fear of man. In the mind, it works something like this: *God wants me to submit. In so doing, I honor him. I will submit because submission is God's idea* (Ephesians 5:21). That's faith, and it greatly pleases your Father (Hebrews 11:6).

Where Things Get Complicated

Submission is fine and wonderful when those in authority ask you to do something you wanted to do anyway. *Hey, no skin off my knees. This submission thing is great!* But what happens when authority asks you to do something that doesn't make sense? Or what if they're just being mean? What happens to submission then?

You've got four options, after which you'd be wise to default to the fifth.

Ask whoever is in charge for an explanation. What you're balking at may look better after a little dialogue. You may have to sell certain people in authority on their *need* to explain—not everyone understands true, caring leadership—but don't demand it.

Samuel, when faced with the potentially fatal mission of anointing David as the next king, humbly questioned God's command. God did not slap Samuel's wrists for asking the question. His explanation freed Samuel to obey in spite of the risks (1 Samuel 16:1-4).

Approach authority with another plan. Assuming you understand what is being asked and why, you have the right to humbly offer a different idea or an alternative suggestion. Daniel gives us a great example of this in action (Daniel 1). But offer the alternative with an open hand, not an iron fist. Submission does not force or manipulate things into place.

Appeal to higher authority. If you don't feel like you're getting a fair hearing, you may decide to go higher up the chain of command. Paul did this while in prison to keep from getting handed over to the Jews who would unjustly kill him (Acts 25:9-11). Realize you may alienate the person whose authority you're skirting. Extend courtesy by advising him of your plan of action: "Sir, I'm afraid I'm going to have to take this up with your superior."

Plead your case as one of submitting to God rather than to men. This is the road you take when authority has asked you to do something in direct opposition to God's Word. But prepare to face the consequences. Peter and his companions did this with great courage when they were forbidden to speak of Jesus Christ (Acts 5:28-29). You'd better be super-sure the situation warrants this approach. Some people are too quick and brazen in claiming God as their only boss.

Submit to what authority says. Failing all of the above, this is your only choice. Accept the hard road, trusting God to overrule if he sees fit. Jesus is the ultimate example of this. Part of him did *not* want to go to the cross. He took his case to the highest Authority, realized his Father would not overrule the plan as it stood, and then accepted the hard road that led to Calvary (Matthew 26:36-46).

God highly honors humble submission in tough situations (Philippians 2:8-9). And you can be very thankful Jesus understood submission. Your salvation depended on it.

Put It on Your Resumé

God isn't against an entrepreneurial spirit. But with great power he *will* resist a proud, unsubmissive heart (James 4:6-7). That's a hard road you don't want to travel.

Learn the secret blessings of submission. You'll make an employee any smart boss would pay a good price to have around.

23

In His Image, Walking Tall
(When self-image doesn't cut it)

Jason checked his new Movado, its gold band and crystal face sparkling in the mirror lights: *5:48 P.M.* In a little over an hour he would dazzle some old friends—in Maggio's Cafe, no less. If he carried himself right, he could have the whole restaurant turning heads. A few might even want to shake his hand.

Jason loved glad-handing. He could work a room like no one else. All those cheery faces, people so glad Jason Bellows was willing to notice them. He had God's gift of backslapping, he was sure. It felt great to make people smile.

He was an up-and-coming lawyer, top of his sophomore class. That's where the Movado came from—a little congratulatory gift from Dad.

He took a deep breath. His lawyerly bearing exuded from his skin like the Polo cologne he had splashed on his face. Better adjust that belt. The golf shirt and pleated pants were Calvin Klein—a little cliché, but no one else could match the cut, at least not on a swelling physique like his.

That fitness membership at Scandinavia's was finally paying off, he decided for the tenth time. A quick flex of a pec sent a ripple through the shirt. Wow, was it ever white, especially against that black marble collar. He wondered if Maggio's used black lights. He should leave the sports jacket at home, just in case. That shirt looked *fine* all by itself.

Tanya and Debbie were going to be there, too. A hopeful thought. It didn't hurt to entertain possibilities about the girls from his former youth group. They never liked him before, but, hey, things change. He'd never had a Movado before, either.

No shortage of girls back at Stanford, but a guy had to beat them off with a stick. They all—every last tempting one of them—had values that made his skin crawl like a bowl full of maggots. He wanted something above the level of "Gotta marry me a rich man—buff between the lats, thick between the lobes (*giggle, giggle*)." Tanya and Debbie were truehearted believers: intelligent, mature, and just plain *nice.* Boy, one of them would sure solve *a lot* of problems.

He picked an imaginary piece of lint off his pants. Those cowboy boots shone. No one else on campus even dared risk looking like a redneck. In spite of his being from Seattle, the boots had earned him the nickname "Jamarillo," an endearing cross between his first name and the Texas town.

He checked once more to make sure there was no sign of last week's gum disaster. What a balloon-popper that had been. *All right, let it go. Positive thoughts. You're the man of the hour. Lord, make it happen, make it* all *happen.*

Stepping into the moist fragrance of an early summer rain, he patted his hair one more time, grateful the clouds were gone. Then he set out, eager and ready to make everyone's day.

Forty-five minutes later he left his car in a far corner of the parking lot near Maggio's. That Toyota Echo of his was a nice ride but not designed to really impress. Dad could have done a little better on that one.

Now, where was that restaurant? He saw its neon sign reflected in the light of a large puddle. *Brace yourselves, gang, I'm here.* Quickly stepping aside to miss a puddle, he was only half conscious of the approaching pickup.

Guuuuuisssssh!

A wall of muddy water leapt from the parking lot. Jason scrambled backwards, his boots clattering dully. The water's main swell fell with a huge splash, fifteen feet beyond the puddle's original border. Jason jumped back another yard. The secondary wave rose and died, harmlessly spitting to within six inches of Jason's pointed, radiant toes.

But two dollops of muddy water arched high in the air. They had hopped from a deep pothole hidden beneath the puddle. As Jason glanced down to make sure his boots were okay, the two drops splattered just below a shoulder, cutting cool, gray trails across the gleaming white material over his right pec.

Jason gasped. Swallowed. And blinked back the tears.

A House of Cards

Anyone whose whole image crumbles under two little beads of water has got some major rethinking to do. Try this passage on for size:

> This is what the Lord says: "Let not the wise man boast of his wisdom, or the strong man boast of his strength, or the rich man boast of his riches, but let him who boasts boast about this: that he understands and knows me, that I am the Lord who exercises kindness, justice and righteousness on earth, for in these I delight."
>
> JEREMIAH 9:23-24

Translation? If what you value most about yourself is your mind, your muscle, or your money, you're living in an emotional house of cards. You will be knocked down ECO—easily, completely, and often.

A Rock Unmoving

You have something totally trustworthy and completely unshakable inside of you. It's the true place where you should build the confidence necessary to face that threatening world out there. What is it?

Your relationship with Jesus Christ.

Think about it. He's the King of kings, Creator of the Universe, Lord of lords. A thunderbolt that would light Chicago for a year is to him mere static. Stars that make our sun look like a golf ball are his to snuff out at a whim. Every single knee will one day humbly bend before the august, irresistible presence of Jesus (Philippians 2:9-10). He is the all-time, big-time boss of everything your mind could imagine (Ephesians 1:21-23).

And he's your friend. Wow. I mean, *Wow!*

Furthermore, Christ's gleaming white righteousness is your very own (2 Corinthians 5:21). Who can muddy that? "If God is for us, who can be against us?" (Romans 8:31).

As you learn to value the solid foundation you have through your relationship with Jesus, you'll be virtually unflappable. See yourself the way God sees you—his creation, his child, his joy, the object of his four-dimensional love (Ephesians 3: 18-19). Bask in the deep security of God's acceptance of you. When you're there, the devil won't be able to throw a tidal wave high enough to touch your soul, let alone rock it.

Need a new image? The image of Christ is yours to enjoy (2 Corinthians 3:17-18). Think about it.

24

Watch Your Eyes
(A chapter mostly for guys)

He stared into the flickering firelight, mouth set in grim determination. Two more tears trickled past his nose as he watched the flames devour the magazine's pages.

That evil mag. As another page curled into black, a picture of glistening skin surfaced, its temptation clearly displayed in spite of the flames. Stabbing the last pages with the poker, he willed the flames to hurry. Then, choking back a sob, he averted his eyes. *Don't look at another one!*

Too late. The sensuous image had seared itself into his memory banks. He closed his eyes and saw her in spite of the dark. Dropping the poker, he crushed two fists against his eyes, determined to squeeze the image out of existence.

He watched as she laughed.

With a long sigh, he gazed back into the flames. *If only I didn't have eyes!*

The answering thought came, clear and gentle: *If only you'd point them at my Son.*

My Story

"I made a covenant with my *eyes* not to look lustfully at a girl" (Job 31:1). I'm not sure about old Job, but I've made a thousand of those promises.

Where to Look?

It started in high school—and it didn't completely go away when I went to Bible college. In my day girls wore jeans so tight that they had to use grease to get them on. Walking through North Park High's crowded halls, I fought to keep my eyes at shoulder level. But that was dangerous. Some of their low-cut sweaters dared me to peek. So I'd aim my eyes higher and concentrate on girls' faces instead. That had its pitfalls, too. Many of them had beautiful eyes. Occasionally they pointed in my direction, along with a smile. Then I was in big trouble.

As a follower of Christ, I couldn't get involved. Romance with someone who didn't love Jesus would have been foolishly blind and against God's clear command: "Do not be yoked together with unbelievers" (2 Corinthians 6:14). I never chased such a relationship, but I desperately wanted to.

Looking Tough

Girls weren't my only eye problem. As one of a handful of Christians in a student body of seventeen hundred, I put up with some ridicule for my faith. It was no big deal, but at the time I thought it was.

In an attempt to ward off snide remarks, I lifted weights and walked as if my chest and chin were fighting for first place. Along with my gorilla walk came my best attempt at a cool gaze, my eyes half closed, determined not to react to anything—even a stupid comment from some subspecies football jock.

That only lasted a few months. God got my attention with his Word: "You bring low those whose *eyes* are haughty" (Psalm 18:27). I decided looking friendly was a better choice.

Looking at Myself

I loved sports. I played a tough match of tennis and a harder game of soccer. But it was in math and science that I really excelled. I once had a teacher say, "Today we're going to have a math competition—Manfred versus the rest of the class." Another time my physics instructor asked me to teach a chapter of our textbook that he himself didn't understand. When I finished, three fellow students told me to keep the teacher's job.

It wasn't bad to be smart, but it shouldn't have gone to my head. "Woe to those who are wise in their own *eyes* and clever in their own sight" (Isaiah 5:21). On that count, I failed big time. Looking in the mirror, I thought I was God's gift to the universe. What a joke.

Trouble Everywhere I Look

I'm struck by how much this world is full of stuff my eyes need to avoid: trash videos, sexy billboards, junk magazines, worthless TV programs. There's no end to the vile garbage that wants to dump itself into my mind. I could go crazy trying to steer clear of it all. Along with Solomon, a man who had a real problem controlling his eyes, I admit, based on experience, that "death and Destruction are never satisfied, and neither are the *eyes* of man" (Proverbs 27:20).

Then there's the bad attitudes that can radiate from my eyeballs: the snotty look, the angry scowl, the I'm-holy-hope-you-are-too expression. How do I handle this vast array of ocular temptation? Am I doomed to all-day guard duty, with my eyes as prisoners? The task seems impossible.

Good thing God specializes in impossibilities.

Where I Should Be Looking

As God's child, I cannot handle a complicated assignment. My heavenly Father knows that, so he simplified the task of controlling my eyes with one small command: "Let us fix our *eyes* on Jesus, the author and perfecter of our faith" (Hebrews 12:2).

We're talking the eyes of my heart here. When they look at my Savior, that's called faith.

As my heart's eyes gaze at Jesus, my physical eyes avoid the many sins they so often stumble into. While I look at him, there's no desire to feast my eyes on some slinky swimsuit calendar ad. With him in focus, my eyes are kind and friendly, not cold and scary. As my soul stares at Christ, I'm too awestruck by his majesty to think much of myself. Simple as that.

But the moment I take my eyes off of him, they start doing foolish things again. And with my eyes pointed elsewhere, things go wrong. Good old Peter is a classic example of that, walking on water until he took his eyes off of Jesus (Matthew 14:25-30).

So my challenge is to learn to look at Christ *consistently*. It's not hard, but it takes practice. My heart's eyes wander as much as my physical ones do, if not more. It takes an ongoing act of faith to keep focusing my soul on him, but it's worth the effort.

I can't tell you what Christ's face looks like—neither can Hollywood, for that matter—but I do know what his heart looks like. His Word describes it to me. The more I read it, the clearer my view of Jesus. What I see is true, noble, right, pure, lovely, admirable, excellent, and praiseworthy (Philippians 4:8. Jesus satisfies my eyes.

He makes me want to keep looking.

25

Watch Your Wardrobe
(A chapter mostly for girls)

Crossing the campus library lawn, she was certain she cut quite a figure. She could feel the heads turning as she walked by. Pretending to pick a stray hair off her shoulder, she caught three of them. Two quickly looked away. One just stood there, gaping.

Pure vanity, she knew, but it felt good.

Oh, my, here he comes. A guy she had yet to catch rubbernecking. Walking straight toward her. *What a smile.* A regular Val Kilmer on a Christian campus. This she had to investigate.

She stopped and touched him on the shoulder. "Hi, can you tell me where the closest entrance to the library is?" *As if I didn't already know.*

He turned, his smile wide. "Yeah, sure. Just over there. See those two green marble pillars? That's where you want to go."

I've never seen whiter teeth. And that thick hair. What color are his eyes?

When she looked to check, what she saw almost made her snarl. His eyes were focused where they really shouldn't have been. Reaching to play with her necklace, she watched the eyes switch to her face. She sensed a trace of embarrassment. *Not nearly enough.*

"My name's Craig. Craig Sanders." The smile now touched his ears. He held out a hand. "What's yours?"

Turning toward the library, she began walking. "I can't remember."

Guys—they're all the same. Every one of them with his mind in the sewer.

A Fresh Take on Modesty

Having made your own wardrobe decisions for perhaps a decade now, you may find it difficult to take an honest look at this subject. That's understandable. For eighteen-plus years you've been fed the line, "If you don't look sexy, you're nothing."

Satan's lies are pretty easy to spot when set down in black and white, aren't they? The problem is, Satan doesn't pawn his lies concerning modesty in bold italics. Instead, he takes a mind and slowly weaves a web in it. Because each thread is so fine, most girls don't notice. Over time Satan casts a thick, crisscrossing pattern, captivating women—even Christians—to his agenda. Eventually many ladies accept standards of dress that, with a little imagination, would make God's angels blush and the devil's demons leer.

God's Concern for You

This problem isn't new. The apostle Paul had to deal with it almost two thousand years ago: "I also want women to dress modestly, with decency and propriety, not with braided hair or gold or pearls or expensive clothes" (1 Timothy 2:9).

Before you toss this book away in disgust, be assured of this: In giving that command, God has your best interests at heart. He's not trying to make life miserable for you. If you're convinced of that, you'll hear him out on the subject.

Modesty is for your own good. Consider these reasons why:

Modesty is safer. Does anyone need to tell you that you live in a world where crimes against women are on the increase? Realize that many men have also been fed a huge line: "If she dresses sexy, she wants it." Enough said.

Modesty doesn't accommodate the devil. Any way you cut it, immodest dress enables Satan to do his job of jerking men around. You don't want that on your conscience. Choose modesty, and we, your brothers in Christ, will salute you with a thankful smile.

Modesty knows no regrets. It takes effort to silence the voice of the Spirit as you slip on that sweater that's just a tad tight, a little low-cut. Moreover, the power sensation that comes with immodest dress is *totally* shallow. Wouldn't it be far more thrilling for your soul to please Jesus with your wardrobe? The apostle Peter, a married man who understood the issues, wrote:

> Your beauty should not come from outward adornment, such as braided hair and the wearing of gold jewelry and fine clothes. Instead, it should be that of your inner self, the unfading beauty of a gentle and quiet spirit, which is of great worth in God's sight. For this is the way the holy women of the past who put their hope in God used to make themselves beautiful.
>
> 1 PETER 3:3-5

No shame in that. And that passage brings up a couple more good points.

Modesty doesn't fade. When the wrinkles finally set in—and they will—you won't be wringing your hands, worried about that oh-so-necessary facelift.

Modesty shines through. God isn't asking you to look frumpy. He wants you to be as beautiful as you can be. True beauty is an inward thing. It can take an otherwise ordinary girl and make her sparkle. In contrast, outward beauty can look pretty ugly on a girl who feels compelled to flaunt it.

Finally, a Good Match

Over the next few years, you will likely be looking for your future husband. As you do, consider this final point: Modesty attracts purity.

Do you want a guy lured in just because some part of you is well endowed? That is a shaky foundation for any relationship. Wouldn't you much rather find someone who loves you for who you are, not for the clothes you wear—or the curves underneath?

None of this is about wearing a refrigerator box for the rest of your life. This is about marrying a godly guy, one who won't be sneaking peeks at the competition—for the rest of your life.

Those godly guys are out there. They're worth the wait.

Take a critical look at your wardrobe and make some wise, God-honoring decisions. Enjoy real beauty.

26

Too Hot to Handle

(Cooling the jets of romantic passion)

"This is where I need to be," she said, arms unraveling, voice thick. "Never been kissed before?"

A shaking thumb wiped moist lips. "A few times." He started the car and flicked on the air, city glitter dim through the foggy windshield. "By my mother."

Throaty laughter. He cringed, face burning. She drew two hearts on the moist glass. He swallowed, folded sweating hands, stared at swaying keys.

Suddenly, with a twist of leg and hip, she lay across his lap. Eyes were lost in shadow, but the moon touched her chin, her neck, her double-hearted locket.

Hands pulled on his arms. "Okay, you big, gorgeous dream. Take me."

The air conditioner purred. The keys stopped swaying.

Gently, firmly, he pushed her back into her own seat. Deaf to a hundred protests, he took her.

Home, where she needed to be.

Reality Check

In real life, it rarely happens that way. When the hormones boil, all reason usually evaporates—just like in the movies. Maybe you've been there, maybe you haven't. Maybe this is a sizzling, current issue for you. Maybe it leaves you stone cold—

a vague possibility you're almost convinced will never come to pass.

Whatever your state, don't consider yourself above temptation. It's worth the time to draw a firm line. Lay it down in writing, out loud, face-to-face—whatever, just make the line clear—before those eyes twinkle, those two hands touch.

Sticking to the Line

You'll need help if you're going to draw the line and make your decision stick. Spend some time meditating on the following biblical warnings. They may save you a world of hurt.

Biblical Passion-Cooler #1

"Flee the evil desires of youth, and pursue righteousness, faith, love and peace, along with those who call on the Lord out of a pure heart" (2 Timothy 2:22). Pursuing peace is important if you truly want purity. When your heart takes its first step toward illicit sex, God's peace will vanish.

Learn to recognize the absence of that peace: the racing heart, the short breath, the pumping hormones. If your passions become unleashed so that your heart knows no peace, you've gone too far. When that tender little goodnight kiss turns into something that has you both groping, step way back and draw a different line. Run from whatever it is that robs you of your peace.

Biblical Passion-Cooler #2

"Abstain from all appearance of evil" (1 Thessalonians 5:22, KJV). Before you crawl into that dark, cozy den, examine your motives for "needing to be alone." Realize that you can enjoy privacy in the center of a busy park.

Learn to appreciate places where temptation has a hard time lurking. And understand that your reputation is easily tainted, even if your purity is maintained. If the gang disappears, leaving the two of you alone in your dorm room over a half box of pizza, grab the box and get out of there. You may think everything is cool; someone else wandering in may decide otherwise.

Biblical Passion-Cooler #3

"Then Amnon hated her with intense hatred. In fact, he hated her more than he had loved her" (2 Samuel 13:15). Read the entire chapter and get the whole sordid story.

Then understand this: The emotions that accompany sexual sin are like Mount St. Helens. You have no idea what direction things will blow, even in your own heart. What "felt so right" can go horribly wrong. Guilt and self-disgust have an ugly tendency to twist, pointing fingers at the one you claimed to cherish.

You'll have even less control over your partner's reactions. There's no predicting the bitter morning after the night before. Make no mistake: With one kiss too many, you could kiss your love good-bye.

Biblical Passion-Cooler #4

"Do not be deceived: God cannot be mocked. A man reaps what he sows. The one who sows to please his sinful nature, from that nature will reap destruction" (Galatians 6:7-8). There's no getting around it: Somehow, some way, sexual compromise will destroy something very precious to you. The principle of reaping what you sow is one hard, fast, ironclad law. You're no exception. You touch something you shouldn't touch before that wedding day, you'll regret it for life. That's true even if you end up marrying that person. The fleeting pleasure of sin now is not worth the scars of disrespect and distrust that come later.

Biblical Passion-Cooler #5

"Flee from sexual immorality. All other sins a man commits are outside his body, but he who sins sexually sins against his own body" (1 Corinthians 6:18). Sex outside of marriage will hurt both you and your partner as no other sin can.

If you lose your wallet, you can replace its contents. If you lose your virginity to a premarital encounter, you've lost part of your soul. If you keep pursuing illicit sex, you could lose your health. Sex outside of God's design is a good thing gone bad.

Biblical Passion-Cooler #6

"Buy the truth and do not sell it; get wisdom, discipline and understanding" (Proverbs 23:23). If you're convinced that sex before marriage is wrong, do you find yourself waffling in the gray areas? Think you can scoop fire into your lap without burning your clothes (Proverbs 6:28)? You need more time in God's Word, "buying truth" on the subject of sexual purity. Do a study on the word *pure* and its derivatives. Meditate on passages like 1 Corinthians 13, Proverbs 5 and 6, and 2 Samuel 11 and 12. When it comes to sex, Hollywood, hell's angels, and high school have cluttered your mind with a writhing mass of lies. Let the water of God's Word course through your soul, washing those lies into the gutter where they belong. Buy the truth.

And once you buy it, hang on tight. Truth disobeyed in one hot encounter is sold for a mere pittance. But like the gift of virginity, truth obeyed knows no price.

27

Still Waiting for Miss Right

(A lesson in contentment)

I was twenty-two, on my way to reach tribal people with the gospel—and still painfully single. High school had seen one serious-but-wasn't-meant-to-be relationship. Bible school gave me a similar lesson or two in heartbreak.

And now I was in missionary training, where the three single ladies who sat with me in class had no intentions of breaking my heart. They were all older than I. One of them was sixty-seven.

So I spent many a spare moment gazing at the training center's bulletin boards, checking out photos of all the missionary babes spread throughout the world and wondering where God would send me.

I think one of them was named Pamela. Nice hair, cute face. I clearly remember that she worked in Papua New Guinea. Wow, did I feel divinely guided to go to Papua New Guinea.

The need for new missionaries in PNG was indeed urgent.

Fifteen months later, still single, I was getting desperate. I still had visions of going to PNG, but a dose of reality had knocked Pamela clear off my radar screen. In fact, my screen was completely empty. I knew without a shadow of doubt that God wanted me in missions, but I was shedding torrents of tears at the thought of going it alone.

It didn't help that I had just wasted three months chasing a relationship with a pretty girl who sort of loved Jesus and had no interest in missions. What was I thinking, asking a wannabe stewardess on a date? She sure was nice to be around, though. Walking away from that one almost disemboweled me.

One day I was hobnobbing with a bunch of missionary candidates, all of them married and with a gaggle of kids. Suddenly there she was, standing in the hallway. Single. Tall. Blonde. Cute nose. A voice that purred. Big eyes. Blue—both of them. And like the others, she was preparing to go to the mission field.

I shook her hand. We talked. I asked her name, offered mine. She smiled. I died. We exchanged another sentence, then checked our watches. She said bye. So did I.

It was over.

The forty-five-second encounter was too far from home to casually pursue, too short to follow up at a distance. I didn't even know her last name. That girl popped into my life only long enough to torture my already bleeding soul.

It was midnight—in more ways than one. And I had a three-hour drive ahead of me.

Her face stared at me the whole way home. Snow swirling around my vehicle, tears gushing out of my eyes, I beat the steering wheel in agony.

"Father! Why?" I screamed into a cold windshield that didn't seem to care. "Why did you even let us *meet*? That was *so* mean. What are you *doing* to me?" I beat the steering wheel some more, my palms aching, my deranged thoughts surprised I hadn't snapped it in two. "Do I have to be a wretched *eunuch* the rest of my life? Is *that* what it's going to take to make you happy? Oh, God, you're killing me!"

My rantings threw me into a fit of coughing and weeping. With slush piling on the road and emotions exploding in my soul, I was in a dangerous way. I didn't care. Right now, the dead end of a snowplow seemed like a great place to be.

Somehow I survived that night, but the questions kept coming: *Is there just one girl out there for me? What if she died at birth? What if she lives in the Ukraine? If not, where is she? Show me! Point me in the right direction. You know I can't go this alone. Send her my way. Throw me at her feet. Please, God, I'm dying.*

The answers I demanded simply wouldn't come. Finally, my heart too weary to rant, I was ready to listen. I think the conversation went something like this:

Child, is my love not enough?

I had to chew on that one. "I'm not sure, Lord. I know it's *supposed* to be, but every time I imagine myself single for the rest of my life, I want to die. So, no, it's not enough."

I'm not asking you to be single for the rest of your life. You're the only one asking that question.

"You mean I don't have to be *willing* to be forever single to make you happy?"

That's right. I've never demanded that willingness from anyone.

"Well, then, what *are* you asking?"

I'm only asking you to be single for the rest of this day.

"You mean, you'll throw me at her feet tomorrow?"

Forget about tomorrow. Just enjoy my love today. That's all you need to worry about.

"In other words, no promises about the future."

Not on this subject, no.

"Hmmm."

That thought needed digesting. Taking the time to accept it, I made another cautious step.

"Okay, let me see. I've tortured myself worrying about tomorrow, envisioning the existence of an unhappy old man who's never known a woman—rather than simply enjoying your love today. Is that what you're saying?"

You're catching on. Now try putting it another way.

It didn't take me long. "I've been asking you for a lifetime of singlehood grace, when you only dole it out in one-day doses."

Exactly. You're there. So, how about it?

"How about what?"

Can you handle being single until the end of today? I ask no more.

To accompany the burst of understanding that flooded my soul, God overwhelmed me with an assurance of his love. Sweet tears in my eyes, I nodded and smiled.

Take a long look at Matthew 6:34. Chisel it in stone. It's the principle you've just come to appreciate. I love you, Manfred.

Opening my Bible, I read these words: "Do not worry about tomorrow, for tomorrow will worry about itself." My mind had seen that line many times, along with the verses that surrounded it. Now it was my heart that was looking.

I was still single, with no guarantees. But the tomorrow questions were gone. Really. The tears didn't stop completely, but the ones that followed were a mere trickle. Jesus replaced the rest by taking me to a whole new level in my relationship with him.

His love is enough. Really. One day at a time.

28

Greater Expectations
(When your dreams die young)

Celine D'Accord ripped a return down the line, sending her opponent sprawling after the ball in an increasingly vain attempt to stay alive. Break point. One more and Celine had game, set, match.

A quick look at Coach gave her some reassurance. He was all smiles and nods. She tried to smile back but failed miserably. That guy held the power of life and death in his face, it seemed. One frown from him, and her tennis scholarship was history. Instead she'd be busing tables to get through university on the quarters and dimes pitched to her by worn out waitresses. *O Lord, no. Please don't let that happen.*

Turning to face her opponent, she saw a fleeting grimace of all-or-nothing determination just before the ball was tossed. Taking a step back, Celine prepared for a hard serve.

This will end now.

The serve tapped the center line. Celine stretched, her forehand barely catching the ball, lobbing it high and deep. She was almost certain it would fall long, but it would be close.

Celine rushed the net.

Watching the ball land just inside the baseline, she rocked on the balls of her feet, ready to react to anything, her racket's shadow falling across the net. The hot passing shot sent her flying to her backhand. As the ball skimmed the net, she stabbed the air, desperate for six more inches, legs flailing behind her. The ball caught the rim of her racket, thudding with a dull smack.

Fighting to regain her balance, Celine watched the ball hop lazily over the net, seeing it bounce twice before passing from view. She vaguely heard the umpire call, "Game, set ...." After that, a white wall of pain covered her like a shroud as she wrapped herself around the umpire's chair.

When Celine opened her eyes, her vision was blurred. She could just make out the clock on the mustard-yellow wall of her hospital room. Her racket arm felt heavy, immobile. Blinking back the fog, she fought to recognize the dark figure that hovered nearby. *O Lord, no. Please don't let this happen.*

It was Coach, gazing at the bent cast before her. He wasn't smiling.

Unclenching the Fist

"In his heart a man plans his course, but the Lord determines his steps" (Proverbs 16:9). It's completely natural for you to have aspirations for the future. If you didn't, you'd be a boulder. The issue is not about *not* having plans.

It's all about how you hold them.

If you hold them tight, they could be torn from your hand in the most painful way. That's particularly true if you allow your plans to swell your head with pride (James 4:13-16). God is a humble God. He simply cannot allow pride to rule in the hearts of his children.

Hold your plans toward heaven on an open palm. When your sovereign God sees fit to change them, it won't be nearly as painful. Proverbs 3:5-6 describes an open-palmed approach: "Lean not on your own understanding; in all your ways acknowledge him, and he will make your paths straight." You've got to believe that God is not a killjoy. Read that again. He wants to fill your heart with more joy than you could imagine. But his way of getting you there often takes a different road than you'd expect:

"For my thoughts are not your thoughts,
neither your ways my ways," declares the Lord.
"As the heavens are higher than the earth,
so are my ways higher than your ways."

ISAIAH 55:8-9

An open palm willingly accepts the higher road. Time to unclench the fist.

Too Many Expectations

When moving into new situations, you probably have the tendency to picture in your mind how you expect things to be. We all do. But rarely does your imagination come anywhere close to reality. With everything from wishing for a spacious bathroom in your dorm to determining the color of your future spouse's hair, expectations have a way of creeping into your soul by the hundreds. Ouch. Not only do you narrow your opportunities—what happens if you meet a lovely redhead?—but also you set yourself up for constant disappointment.

This gets really complicated when you start having expectations of people's actions. If you expect Frank to buy lunch because you bought last time, what happens if he forgets? Depending on the intensity of your expectation, you may decide never to have lunch with him again. *The mooch.* Or what if Caroline doesn't come to the Bible study you prepared so hard for? Will your expectations drive you into *coercing* her to come the next time? Is that what you want?

Your expectations will be unwanted weights if heaped on people's heads. They'll make you a heavy person to be around.

A less painful, less limiting, less alienating approach is found in Psalm 62:5: "My soul, wait thou only upon God; for my expectation is from him" (KJV). Rather than harboring a host of foolish expectations, a personal agenda that is way too long, expect Jesus to give you the grace to face life as it comes. Let him teach you flexibility and patience, filling your life with open acceptance, quiet approachability, and smooth transitions.

That's the life Jesus himself enjoyed. Think of all the people who clamored for his time, his healing touch, or his wisdom. He calmly handled it all as it came, person by person, with no selfish agenda. He never manipulated, never flew into a flap. He was so approachable that children loved to hover around his knees. His only expectation was to please his Father— wherever that took him (John 8:29).

That's the life Jesus wants you to enjoy—a life of simple but great expectations.

29

Making Sense Out of Suffering
(When hard times won't quit)

Looking back, my early Christian years—Bible college included—were lived on a rather superficial plane. As long as things went smoothly, I felt great, Jesus was cool, church was wonderful, ministry rocked, and the whole anguished world smiled because I was so happy.

That was a rare feeling.

The spine-jarring bumps in the road of life were far more common. With few exceptions, they all knocked me flying, leaving me an emotional basket case tumbling into the ditch of disappointment, disillusionment, and discouragement.

At the admittedly ancient age of thirty-three, I finally learned some huge and indispensable truths, things that now enable me to more wholesomely process life's inevitable hard spots. It's my simple prayer that God gives you the grace to learn these things far sooner than I did. I wouldn't want anyone to be as slow on the uptake as I have been.

My Story of Suffering

It started with the rats and constant lack of water. Beth and I were now full-time missionaries living in a desert mountain town where the rodents thrived a whole lot better than we mere humans—they didn't need as much water. Our days seemed filled with nothing but sloshing buckets and filthy traps. Sleepless nights were spent to the sound of our Tupperware being chewed to shreds. Those nuisances soon became the least of our worries.

The wild gunfire really caught us off guard. Our next-door neighbors loved the sound of machine guns—at about 2:00 A.M. every other night. One time, in the middle of the day, several stray bullets ricocheted in our direction—we heard them buzz by. On another occasion, someone shot over my head—his way of warning me he was not in a visiting mood.

Then came the suspicious, callous nature of the people to whom God had called us. Abused for centuries by outsiders, the Pima had grown a thick shell of cold stoicism. Even among themselves they were unfriendly. Deep conversations consisted of the weather, the new red truck in town, or what day of the week it was.

I once asked a Pima, "Do you enjoy hunting?" He took two steps back and growled, "What are you asking me *that* for?" I had crossed the threshold of "too personal." Another time I chatted with a friend, meeting all the small-talk requirements before venturing, "You have a Bible, don't you? Have you ever read the Gospel of John?" His response: "It sure is cold these days, isn't it?"

In the midst of all these adjustments, one bright moment filled us with joy. Beth was pregnant, the answer to seven years of prayer. We talked about names and did all the things that expectant parents do. We envisioned the child being used by God to open Pima hearts. Before the end of the first trimester, the good news turned to tragedy. Our hopes of a child vanished.

Our despair and confusion were absolute. We went the gamut of self-pity, anger, and remorse. We asked "Why?" a thousand times without a single, solid answer. Although we never entertained specific thoughts of leaving the mission field, we wanted to quit. We didn't even consider quitting our ministry to the Pima—we wanted to say good-bye to Christianity altogether.

I remember praying, tears pouring down my face, *"Lord, you promised us abundant life. Well, this isn't. It's pure misery."*

Disappointed, disillusioned, and discouraged, I could make no sense of my suffering.

The Sooner Accepted, the Better
In seeking to process my misery, I realized that a certain unfulfilled expectation lurked within me: I wanted life to be hassle-free. *No problems allowed, God, thank you.* Theoretically I knew that was a silly wish. Even Jesus made it clear that my desires were pure fantasy, something to be reserved for heaven alone: "Here on earth you will have many trials and sorrows" (John 16:33, NLT). But those were words I wasn't willing to consider on anything but the most superficial level.

Deep down where it counts, I demanded smooth sailing. When I didn't get what I wanted, my soul threw a royal, spitting, red-faced tantrum. Disgust, disrespect, and disobedience would fill me.

Something had to give. It certainly wasn't God who needed to change. His Son had done everything possible to prepare me for the reality of life on earth— *"Here on earth you will have many trials and sorrows"*—but it took quite a while for me to accept it. When I finally faced truth squarely, it was time for my next lesson.

Not God's Fault

It slowly became clear to me that every bump in the road caused me to question God's goodness. *There he goes again, zapping me. Can't that Old Man with the lightning bolts in his hand give it a rest?*

Satan had used my trials to paint an ugly picture of the God who loved me. It was a picture so hideous that I wasn't willing to admit it was there, lurking in my heart. I was a missionary. Missionaries aren't supposed to have bad ideas about the God they serve. It took a dear friend to show me how twisted my thinking had become.

Realizing my need for a fresh view of God, I humbly but openly confessed the distorted image I had carried so long: *You know, God, I really think you're an ogre. I know that's wrong, but that's just where I'm at. If this is going to change, you're going to have to help me.*

I never sensed God's censure, never felt like, *Oops, he's really taking this personally.* He knew the enemy had pulled the wool over my eyes. And he was most gentle in pulling it back, allowing me to agree with the psalmist's view of God: "You are good, and what you do is good" (Psalm 119:68). With tiny baby steps, I inched toward the truth of that verse. God is all good, no bad. I needed to believe that in a place where it really mattered.

Part of what helped get me there was understanding the true fountainhead of all the bad things that happen in this world: *sin.* You would think that a Bible school graduate would have been able to figure that one out far sooner. But I hadn't— at least not where it could touch me.

Sin is not God's fault. It was never his will to see sin enter the world, nor does he enjoy seeing mankind suffer under it (Ezekiel 18:23).

Sin hurts everyone, even the "good guys"—God's children. Sin's consequences attack us from every side, from within and without. What we suffer is not merely the result of our personal sin. The sin of others can reach out and slash us in the most devastating ways. Drunk drivers kill families, then walk away. HIV-tainted transfusions infect innocent people, giving them an unjust death sentence. And little babies miscarry, simply because Adam and Eve couldn't resist.

Sin is a horrible thing. Sin is at fault for all our suffering (Romans 5:12). Sin is the ever-present ogre in our every waking nightmare.

Not God.

It was about time I pointed my accusations in the right direction.

Tough Times Pay

Having accepted that trials were inevitable this side of heaven, that God was truly good, and that sin was the source of all my hurts, I still needed more hope. Even though God wasn't at fault, suffering just because I *had to* wasn't in the least appealing.

The next lesson was straightforward: "Blessed is the man who perseveres under trial, because when he has stood the test, he will receive the crown of life that God has promised to those who love him" (James 1:12). Wow! Suffering now had purpose and meaning. It gave me the opportunity to win something truly *valuable*. All I needed was a God-loving perseverance, something Jesus would gladly give me if I looked to him (Hebrews 12:1-3). It was time to stop muttering and start suffering graciously.

With more study, I discovered the dividends of suffering get even better: "If we suffer, we shall also reign with him" (2 Timothy 2:12, KJV). Those words were written by a man who was within hours of having his head chopped off. Paul knew what he was talking about. He willingly suffered as a courageous missionary in a host of ways (2 Corinthians 11:23-28). He now will enjoy the great privilege of reigning with Jesus as one of Christendom's chief statesmen. I realized that the same opportunity could be mine—if I learned to handle suffering as God would have me.

I know this will sound bad, but I still wasn't satisfied. A big crown in heaven and a chance to reign with Jesus wouldn't do much for me here on earth. Wasn't there something that could make suffering pay dividends right now?

Better believe it.

Suffering Gives a Person Depth

The conclusion seems inevitable: *There is something shallow about a soul that has never really suffered.* If there are deep souls out there who haven't been greatly wounded by life in a sinful world, I haven't met them.

I've met a *lot* of people.

The ones that strike me as sincere, God-fearing, Jesus-loving, Spirit-filled people invariably have suffered deeply in some way. I know because I ask a lot of questions when I meet those kinds of people. The details are different, but the conclusion is always the same: "We've learned to accept suffering as something God uses in our souls."

Most of the time, there's one passage that arises in that kind of conversation:

> Praise be to the God and Father of our Lord Jesus Christ, the Father of compassion and the God of all comfort, who comforts us in all our troubles, so that we can comfort those in any trouble with the comfort we ourselves have received from God.
>
> 2 CORINTHIANS 1:3-4

Translation? Until I've suffered myself and allowed God to comfort me in it, I'm not going to be much comfort to anyone else. Allowing God to comfort me is key. If I go through suffering without enjoying God's comfort, I'll come away bitter. A bitter soul is no comfort to anyone.

But having enjoyed God's comfort, I can pass that comfort on to the many around me who also suffer. In the wake of a shattered World Trade Center—and the events that follow—there will be no shortage of people to comfort.

"Here on earth you will have many trials and sorrows."

This once-shallow soul is no longer so afraid of suffering. I want to encourage people in the midst of hard times. If hard times are what it takes for me to learn true encouragement, I'm ready to pay the price.

Suffering finally makes sense.

30

Jesus, Your Major for Life

(Entering into abundance)

You've chosen the right road, of that you're sure. It's a narrow one, with deep ditches lining both sides, but the sky shines brightly, and road signs mark the way, so you're fine. You walk along joyfully, enjoying the scenery, reading the signs. This is a great road.

But the signs begin to multiply.

It's gradual at first—an extra sign here or there, full of directions on how to walk the road before you. You pause to read each sign, then move forward, determined to follow the growing list of guidelines. You really want to travel this journey well.

But the signs keep coming.

You watch little men feverishly constructing large billboards, all in a rush to finish before you pass by. Where the billboards stand completed, men in gray suits frantically beckon, each pointing to his sign. Some begin to yell, insisting their notice, their warning, is more important than the rest.

You listen, you read, but you can no longer absorb.

Where the signs once stood well back from the road, they now hover close, leaning with menace, muscling each other for more space. The shadows they cast block out the sun. Once lovely scenery is now smothered in a web of posts, arrows, and broken-down placards.

You're still convinced this is the right road, but the journey is no longer joyful. You sit down, one foot dangling into the ditch. You cover your ears and close your eyes. You need a rest.

At the very best moment, his hand touches your shoulder. You open your eyes. His smile greets you. His other hand offers to lift you to your feet. You feel the scars as you stand, convinced you know this Person, suddenly most aware that you want to know him more.

You continue your journey with him beside you. You ask him about all the signs.

One by one, he points out the necessary ones, the ones he himself ordered. He explains their meaning, the good things each sign holds in store. These few road markers move back to their proper place. And as he speaks, the other signs—the useless ones, the scary ones—slowly fade away.

The sun shines again. The scenery is more beautiful than ever. Your joy returns.

This is a great road.

Rules Versus Relationship

What comes to your mind when you think of the Christian life? If the answer is, *Rules, rules, and more rules,* you're not a happy person. If, on the other hand, your heart's response is, *Abundant life through a relationship with Jesus,* you'll be enjoying the journey.

In all likelihood you're somewhere between the two—right there with the rest of us. Some days the Christian life appears difficult, seemingly not worth the effort. On other days you're excited about Jesus, ready to go wherever he sends you and to do whatever he asks.

Here are a few things to consider so that those hard days are kept to a minimum:

Jesus' expressed goal is to give you abundant life.

"I have come that they might have life, and have it to the full" (John 10:10). When you consider that Christ created the universe, it is an awesome thought to realize that his current great purpose is to enable you to enjoy real life.

One of the best things you can do to join him in that effort is be quick to admit when life is miserable. *Jesus, I know you want me to enjoy life to the full, but it's not working right now. Can you give me a new perspective? Where have I taken a wrong turn? Bring me back to abundance, please.* A sincere prayer like that is something Jesus never tires of. It's his job to answer those prayers.

Jesus himself is your life.

"When *Christ, who is your life,* appears, then you also will appear with him in glory" (Colossians 3:4). It is wrong to think of God sending down one-a-day multivitamin dosages of "life," as if life were an entity in itself, dispensed in little bottles. *Jesus* is your life. When you ask for more reality in your spiritual life, God will respond by giving you more of his Son. So every time you pray, *God, I'm not experiencing abundant life,* expect to receive a fresh view of Jesus.

Death opens the door to more of Jesus' life.

"We always carry around in our body the death of Jesus, so that the life of Jesus may also be revealed in our body" (2 Corinthians 4:10). God uses the difficult things in life to reveal where ugly self still takes center stage. While taking you through the sometimes painful process, God reminds you that self has no right to call the shots, that you're dead, and that true life is in Jesus. Don't resist or try to escape what God seeks to do. Allow God to teach you what your death with Christ means, so that you may enjoy more of his life (Galatians 2:20).

Obey Jesus as a friend.

"You are my friends if you do what I command" (John 15:14). Don't divorce Christ's commands from your relationship with him. Cold obedience to a list of written rules is a joyless existence. See yourself doing what you do because your best friend has asked it of you. Then do it with your whole heart. There's no better way to say, *"I love you, Jesus"* (1 John 5:3).

For true freedom, shackle yourself to Jesus.

Satan continually pawns the lie that freedom is found only through complete independence from others. In the ears of many a college freshman, he whispers, "You're away from home now, so the chains are gone. You're free to do what you want. Have at it." But true freedom is found in these words from Jesus: "Take my yoke upon you and learn from me, for I am gentle and humble in heart, and you will find rest for your souls. For my yoke is easy, and my burden is light" (Matthew 11:29-30).

Whatever your major in university or college, your major for life is Jesus.

"I want to know Christ and the power of his resurrection and the fellowship of sharing in his sufferings, becoming like him in his death, and so, somehow, to attain to the resurrection from the dead" (Philippians 3:10-11). If you wholeheartedly walk the road with him, Jesus will take you from infancy to maturity, from mediocrity to excellence, from folly to wisdom, from sin to service, from misery to joy.

From Death to Life

If you'll let him, Jesus will take you from death to life. This isn't about the body and breathing. This is about your spirit and the quality of your earthly existence. It's about abundant life.

I want to know Christ. Study him long. Learn from him well.

Manfred Koehler:
Who is he?

Real job: Missionary to the Pima Indians of northwestern Mexico.

Favorite organization: New Tribes Mission.

Best friend: Jesus.

Other best friend: His wife of fifteen years, Beth.

Languages spoken: Spanish (el idioma del cielo), Pima (si'i la'asim no'ok), German (meine eldern sind deutsch, aber ich habe schon beinah alles vergessen), and English (with a Canadian accent, eh!).

Writing gigs: *Breakaway* since 1993, *Brio* since 1996, *Discipleship Journal, Clubhouse, Clubhouse Jr., LifeWise, Physician, Power for Living, Moody*—and more.

Other interests: photography (look out, *National Geographic*), chess (on his new Handspring Visor), half marathons (with Beth alongside all the way), tennis (rushing the net any chance he gets), and speaking at young people's retreats (where everyone is *hungry* for Jesus).

Areas he's about to explore: Web site design, digital photography, principles of leadership (without being bossy), in-depth Bible study (without getting bored), and intercessory prayer (without getting distracted).

Favorite books of all time:
Principles of Spiritual Growth, by Miles Stanford.
The Hobbit, by J.R.R. Tolkien.
The Normal Christian Life, by Watchman Nee.
The Chosen, by Chaim Potok.
Practicing His Presence, by Brother Lawrence and Frank Labauch.
Endurance: Shackleton's Legendary Antarctic Expedition, by Caroline Alexander.
Christ-Centered Preaching, by Bryan Chapell.

Most scrumptious food choice: Chicken fajitas with lots of cheese and hot salsa, washed down with ice-cold Mountain Dew.

A Web site he wants you to check out: <www.MajoringInLife.com>.